W9-CAE-444

"Many Americans, surveys reveal, are eager to have an encounter with the living God, yet too often feel sidetracked by concern over such questions as: Is God really approachable? What do I say when I pray? Tim Jones addresses such concerns with clarity and freshness, enabling readers to come closer to realizing their heartfelt desire to hear and serve God."

> —George Gallup Jr.
> George H. Gallup International Institute

"I often shrink from books about prayer, because they usually produce in me feelings of inadequacy. I was delighted to find Tim Jones to be a sympathetic, not intimidating, guide. He writes with humility, clarity, and practicality—exactly the qualities I want in a book on prayer."

> —Philip Yancey
> Author of *Where Is God When It Hurts*
> and *The Jesus I Never Knew*

"If you seek change, and joy, and conviction, read Tim's book. It will make a profound difference in your spiritual life."

> —Christopher de Vinck
> Author of *The Power of the Powerless*
> and *Only the Heart Knows How to Find Them*

"Prayer, the expression of our deepest and most essential self, also names our most pervasive inadequacy. And so we need guides, men and women who return us to our true selves and encourage us to do what is most natural to us. Timothy Jones is a reassuring guide: he guides us into a life of prayer not by cramming us with knowledge and technique, but by quietly returning us to simplicity of soul and the presence of God."

> —Eugene H. Peterson
> James Houston Professor of Spiritual Theology
> Regent College, Vancouver, BC

CH

The Art of Prayer

A Simple Guide

TIMOTHY JONES

Ballantine Books
New York

All rights reserved under International and Pan-American Copyright Conventions. Published in the United States by Ballantine Books, a division of Random House, Inc., New York, and simultaneously in Canada by Random House of Canada Limited, Toronto.

Grateful acknowledgment is made to the following for permission to reprint previously published material:

Chosen Books: Excerpt from *Adventures in Prayer* by Catherine Marshall, 1985. Reprinted by permission of Chosen Books, a division of Baker Book House Company, Grand Rapids, Michigan.

Hodder & Stoughton Ltd.: Excerpt from *New Parish Prayers* by Frank Colquhoun. Reprinted by permission of Hodder & Stoughton Ltd.

Paragon House: Excerpts from *Voices of Silence* by Frank Bianco. Reprinted by permission of Paragon House.

Simon & Schuster and A. P. Watt Ltd: Excerpt from "Crazy Jane Talks with the Bishop" by W. B. Yeats, reprinted from *The Poems of W. B. Yeats: A New Edition* by Richard J. Finneran. Published in Great Britain in *The Collected Poems of W. B. Yeats.* Copyright © 1933 by Macmillan Publishing Company, renewed 1961 by Bertha Georgie Yeats. Reprinted by permission of Simon & Schuster and A. P. Watt Ltd., on behalf of Michael Yeats.

Scripture taken from the Holy Bible, New International Version® NIV®. Copyright © 1973, 1978, 1984 by International Bible Society. Used by permission of Zondervan Publishing House. All rights reserved.

http://www.randomhouse.com

Library of Congress Cataloging-in-Publication Data
Jones, Timothy K., 1955–
The art of prayer : a simple guide / Timothy Jones.
p.   cm.
ISBN 0-345-40041-0
1. Prayer—Christianity.   2. Jones, Timothy K., 1955–   .   I. Title.
BV215.J67 1997
248.3'2—dc21   96-48003
                                                                              CIP

Text design by Holly Johnson
Cover design by Min Choi

Manufactured in the United States of America

First Edition: April 1997
10 9 8 7 6 5 4 3 2 1

CH   7/97

To Jill, with love

Contents

Acknowledgments

In the writing of this book scores of people have fed me their insights through informal conversations, interviews, correspondence, and even Internet postings. Their struggles, experiences, and insights have enriched this book wonderfully. While most of them go unnamed, their comments appear throughout this book. I am grateful for their sharing.

I also thank those who have read and offered comments on early drafts, including Kevin Miller, Peter Shockey, Ken Abraham, and especially my wife, Jill Zook-Jones. My heartfelt thanks also to my editor, Elizabeth Zack, for her superb editorial skills, and to the entire Ballantine team.

The Art of
Prayer

Introduction:
The First Steps

At the profoundest depths of life, people talk not about God but with him.

—D. ELTON TRUEBLOOD

My soul thirsts for You.

—KING DAVID OF ISRAEL

Prayer is capturing our imaginations like never before. This week more of us will pray than will exercise, go to work, or have sex.[1] Talk to executive or mechanic, teenager or retiree, churchgoer or skeptic, and you find phenomenal interest in things spiritual. A friend of mine calls it an ache for cosmic specialness. No longer will mere belief in something "out

3

there" do. We want to talk to God. Experience God first-hand. "You have made us for yourself," prayed Augustine centuries ago, "and our heart is restless until it rests in you."[2] Something tells us he was right.

I think of my sister-in-law in New Jersey. She has little interest in church and traditional Christianity, yet she finds herself praying. "Sometimes when I see something beautiful—a baby laughing, the sun coming up—I feel moved to give a short prayer. I say 'Thank you, Lord.' " Such wonderful moments tug at something deep within. As I look back over my forty years of life, I realize how often such experiences have prompted me to pray.

Life's big crises and little anxieties also make us long for satisfying prayer: Grieving and smarting from a divorce, hearing an ominous report from a medical test, seeing our children riding bumpily through adolescence—such moments drive us to pour out our souls to Someone beyond ourselves. In times like these it's hard *not* to pray. Ellen Gulden, the main character in Anna Quindlen's *One True Thing*, watches her cancer-ridden mother receive chemotherapy "drop by drop by please-let-it-work-God drop." What does she do?

"Oh yes, I prayed in that [hospital] cubicle and in the hallway outside and in the cafeteria, where I went as much to shake the feeling of being buried alive . . . as much as because I really wanted another cup of coffee. But I prayed to myself without form, only inchoate feelings, one word: please, please, please, please."[3]

That we realize we are attracted to prayer does not mean we feel we are particularly good at it. For all of our inclination to pray, many of us are still searching for *how*. Or if we have some know-how, we still sense that we're missing something. Other people's experiences with God somehow seem more fulfilling than our own. Sometimes our prayers seem no more satisfying than Ellen's blurted feelings.

Most of us want to find a way of praying that gives our lives richness and hope. When we talk to God, can we do better than stammer? Can we move beyond rote repetition or stale habit? Is it possible to pray with confidence? Can time spent with God transform us?

When I was growing up in Southern California, we "said grace" at meals. I was vaguely aware that my parents prayed at other times, away from the dinner table. My father told me once about a moving experience on a New England hillside when he was overtaken by an amazing awareness of God's presence. He said he was never the same afterward. My mother told me how prayer and her rural Tennessee Methodist roots kept her going through a miscarriage, through colon cancer, through everyday life. And every week, Sunday school and church were part of our family's routine. Prayer was assumed in our house, and I learned much from my parents' example. But we rarely talked about prayer, and almost never about how to *do* it.

I went on to major in religious studies in college and then complete a master's degree in pastoral studies from Princeton Theological Seminary, one of the world's finest theological schools. But even there I was largely on my own when it came to the actual encounter of my soul with God. Apart from some notable exceptions—a pastor here, a professor there—few people offered consistent spiritual guidance. I felt strongly attracted to prayer, but I questioned and struggled, mostly alone.

If you are like me, several questions or concerns bother you when you decide to move from mere attraction to serious practice. As I have reflected on my own praying, talked to scores of friends, and ransacked countless books, I have found that the following questions make many of us hesitate:

- *Is God really approachable?* Like Dorothy and her ragamuffin band on their way to Oz, we may need to find courage to come near God. We may feel unworthy, and our fears drive a wedge between us and whatever picture we have of God. We conclude that God will keep us at arm's distance. I am amazed at how many people I have heard say they do not feel "good enough" to pray—even people who have prayed and attended church for years. They suspect God won't like them, let alone love them. For many of us some sin, a lifetime of spiritual apathy, the fear we haven't "measured up," even the feeling that we haven't prayed enough may leave us thinking God holds himself back. We need to know, Will God greet me when I come?
- *Does God listen carefully?* "For so many years," a woman confessed to her counselor and spiritual mentor, "there had

been a high, impenetrable wall between God and myself. I used to throw my little gifts over the wall and hope that someone was on the other side receiving them. It was impersonal, unsatisfying, but I thought it was the best I could do or even hope for."[1] We may think we can expect no better. But for prayer to seem real, we need a God who is vividly, personally present. We want to know God will pay attention.

• *What do I say when I pray?* How do I find the actual words? Are there certain words or phrases we need to use in prayer to get it "right"? Vaguely remembered lines from church or synagogue rituals help some of us. Maybe you have mimicked others or experimented enough to have fashioned a makeshift formula for praying. A friend of mine, admitting his feeling of inadequacy in prayer, once confessed, "I try to use big-sounding theological words when I pray because I'm afraid God won't hear me otherwise." Prayer sometimes seems like a complicated enterprise reserved for mystics, for those who have time to trek to mountaintop retreats or learn the catchphrases of the religious professionals. We hope it can be simpler than all that.

• *I used to feel closer to God; can I get that feeling back?* If you were raised in a practicing religious household, the problem may not be lack of words or belief so much as a loss of spiritual energy. You don't doubt the great tenets of faith and devotion as much as sense that your soul needs reviving. You feel spiritually cold. You'd like to see your faith thaw, warm, and perhaps even catch fire. As hurried and harried as your schedule is, you realize that nothing less than heartfelt faith will keep you going in the practice of prayer.

- *Will God respond to my prayers?* We hear stories of someone who claims that God got them or a loved one out of a jam because they prayed. Or we read a book like *Healing Words: The Power of Prayer and the Practice of Medicine*; author Larry Dossey, former chief of staff at Medical City Dallas Hospital, cites scores of studies of how prayer benefits patients with high blood pressure, heart attacks, and injuries.[5] But the research does not always jibe with our daily experiences, or at least our feelings. Will we see such spectacular results when we pray? We have all sincerely, desperately pleaded for some release from a prison of pain or illness, some hoped-for promotion or reprieve, only to experience disappointment with God's response. What if God seems to turn a deaf ear?

I believe that the answers to all our questions about prayer are ultimately quite simple. That is where this book can help. Our not knowing exactly how prayer works need not keep us from its delights. That we fumble for words does not disqualify us. Prayer is for nonexperts. It is possible—and important—for the person with the slightest stirring of spiritual interest to begin to pray. Prayer can be wonderfully uncomplicated. Indeed the working title for this book at the beginning was *Prayer Made Simple*.

A book on prayer, I should also underline, is not like a book on chemistry or carpentry. Talking to God is more art than science, more a relationship than a set of techniques. It asks us to listen to our hearts as much as to our heads. It involves our deepest selves and our most everyday moments.

So while plumbing the depths of prayer can take a lifetime, while prayer is not always easy, it can be as simple as talking to a caring friend. A forty-something man who had for years wandered amid a salad bar of spiritualities once wrote me: "I have a feeling my prayer life is shifting into high gear these days. I'm learning how to talk to God again in plain old words." At its barest definition, prayer is simply the language of relationship between us and God. We can use simple words from the heart. "In the morning, O Lord," penned a Psalm writer centuries ago, "you hear my voice; in the morning I lay my requests before you and wait in expectation" (Psalm 5:3 NIV).

The other day I heard a minister talk about being "hungry" for God. The expression is really quite odd. Hunger has a very earthy side—a rumbling stomach, an impulse to chew, a desire to be satisfied. But my friend was on to something. When we do not eat, gnawing appetite drives us to the refrigerator; when we neglect our soul hunger, or fill it with spiritual junk food, we know we need something more.

And that hunger therefore tells us something. It is a cause for hope.

"I know," writes Henri Nouwen, "that the fact that I am always searching for God, always struggling to discover the fullness of Love, always yearning for complete truth, tells me that I have already been given a taste of God, of Love and of Truth. I can only look for something that I have, to some degree, already found."[6] That we want to pray suggests we can. That we want to pray suggests that there is someone waiting for us to speak, waiting to listen. There is no mysterious key to open up the riches of prayer. The desire to pray itself is all we need to start. "We approach God through love, not navigation," Augustine once wrote. Not through charts and lists and abstractions, but with a simple heart. In our seeking we can be found. In our reaching out we will be met.

Prayer, then, begins with whoever I am, wherever I may be, whatever I can give. You are ready to begin praying the moment you sense that there is something more to life and to faith than you now know. You won't want to—you don't need to—stop there. But such talking to God, simple and stuttering as it may be, can lead to a relationship far beyond what you may have ever thought possible. This book can help make that possibility a reality.

Prayers

Lord, you stir [us] to take pleasure in praising you, because you have made us for yourself, and our heart is restless until it rests in you.

—AUGUSTINE[7]

Father in heaven, when the thought of you wakes in our hearts, let it not wake like a frightened bird that flies about in dismay, but like a child waking from its sleep with a heavenly smile.

—SØREN KIERKEGAARD[8]

Help us, Lord, to turn toward you, and in our turning, find that you have been turned toward us all along. Amen.

Part One

How We Approach God

1

A Cry for
Help

*I have been driven many times to my knees by the over-
whelming conviction that I had nowhere else to go. My
own wisdom, and that of all about me, seemed insuffi-
cient for the day.*

—ABRAHAM LINCOLN

*It does not need to be a formal prayer: the most stum-
bling and broken cry—a sigh, a whisper, anything that
tells the heart's loneliness and need and penitence—can
find its way to him.*

—PHILLIPS BROOKS

Never will I forget the terror of one night several years ago.
My wife and family and I lived in a second-story apartment

in a midwest suburb. It would have been a typical bedtime, except that my sons couldn't seem to get settled. As they jumped out of their bunk bed to use the bathroom one more time, the thudding sound of their small feet on the floor infuriated our downstairs neighbor, whose bedroom must have been directly below theirs. He flew into a rage, scaling the stairs outside our hallway.

"Open this door," he screamed, "or I'll kill you!"

With images of a fist or worse in my face, I refused. He ran back down the steps and out into the black-topped parking lot below our window. There he stood, yelling and bellowing his threats.

With trembling hands I punched 911 for help. But just as intently and instinctively, I prayed. I don't recall what I said to God, but my words surely made up in urgency what they lacked in eloquence. By the time the police came and eventually settled our neighbor down, we had gathered as a family to pray out loud. Through trembling words the kids uttered prayers beautiful in directness and simplicity: "Lord, keep us safe. Help us!"

Many of my prayers over the years have been hatched in similarly needy times. A job I have eagerly wanted, a hurt in the wake of a friend's snub, a doctor's frown over a medical test on my wife—such moments make me eager to find resources beyond my own. Need often prompts me to turn to God. Just a little while ago, in fact, worries about a project at work kept waking me up in the wee hours. As I lay in bed those dark mornings, I found in my worry great energy and motivation to pray. Time and again the things that stress and trouble me have made me a praying man. They have schooled me in the art of prayer.

But occasionally I wonder, *Shouldn't prayer have to do with loftier things?* I notice how often my praying chronically grows out of daily concerns—my career, our family budget, my children's health. Does God mind if I come with my anxieties and everyday misfortunes? "I've been committed to God for twenty years," a close friend once admitted, "and have long heard the idea that I should always begin my praying with thankfulness and adoration of God. But try as I might to do differently, I enter prayer with things that burden me."

That makes many of us uncomfortable. Some people are so uneasy that they conclude that prayer prompted by need belongs to preschool piety. We should "outgrow" the impulse to come to God for "favors" or help. People even make fun of such praying, lumping it with the sentiment of the Janis Joplin song that asks God to buy her a Mercedes-Benz because her friends all drive Porsches. Only the selfish or spiritually immature will turn to God in need, we hear others say. So we hesitate to come to God with what bothers us.

Years of praying have convinced me that these fears are ungrounded. It bothers me less and less that my needy moments drive me to prayer. None of us coasts through life without sometimes needing help. Who among us always has enough smarts and stamina and insight to get by? So we often must look outside ourselves. And at precisely those moments we may be spiritually open like never before. We let our needs drive us to God.

As we do, we will discover several realities about prayer.

Prayer Begins Where We Are, Not Where We Think We Should Be

Perhaps no other conviction has done more to free me to turn to God. I come "just as I am," as an old gospel hymn has it. "Pray as you can, not as you can't," said one wise spiritual teacher.[1] If that means my prayers are earthy or needy, so be it. If I come somewhat desperately, God understands.

Many of the prayers I read in the Bible are rough-edged and unrefined to an astonishing degree, even to the point of asking God to take revenge on an enemy. They sometimes make me wince. But seeing such raw intensity reminds me that I can blurt out my words in panic or in pain, not just when I am feeling holy. God wants *me*. I do not put on airs or try to give myself a spiritual makeover to talk to God. I turn my worries into cries for help. I let my fears nudge me to God.

Brother Giles, one of the earliest followers of Francis of Assisi in the twelfth century, once told of a shy peasant woman whose only son had been arrested for a crime. As the boy was being led away to be hanged, Giles asked, would not that woman, although shy and simple, scream, with disheveled hair and bared breast, and run to ask the king to free her son? Who—I ask you—taught that simple woman to make a petition for her son? Did not necessity and her love for her son make that shy woman (who previously hardly went beyond the threshold of her house) almost daring, running and screaming through the streets among men? And did it not make a simple person wise? Just so he who truly knew his own evils, dangers, and losses would be able to pray well—and would want to do so.[2]

As with that woman, reaching out in need may make our praying real. Our praying will go beyond formalities. We might finally get honest about what makes us tick, or who ticks us off. It will be the real "I" who speaks. It is no accident that Jesus prayed and sweated "drops of blood" the night before he faced death on the cross. In the same way it is not surprising to find ourselves driven desperately closer to God in times of trouble.

And the need that drives us to prayer, I find, is not just desperate, and not just the alarm of crisis. Boring sameness plagues as many of us as emergency. We also cry out for help in the flat stretches of life when not much exciting seems to happen, when we give up hope for change. That restlessness can turn us outside of ourselves also.

Which leads to a second reality about prayer.

Prayer Thrives in the Soil of Daily Realities, Not Just in the Stratosphere of Devotion

We live lives of little things, I once heard someone say. And because God cares about the details, because he knows that daily commutes and dirty diapers and mortgage payments and drawn-out divorces consume our waking hours, praying embraces these things. "Anything large enough for a wish to light upon," said nineteenth-century writer George Mac-Donald, "is large enough to hang a prayer on."[3]

Spirituality does not cut us off from the concrete daily-ness of our lives. I like the title of a spiritual classic: *The Sacrament of the Present Moment.* In the corners of the everyday—even the bland and monotonous—we find traces of the sacred. Where we are is where we pray. Why try to begin at any other place?

But perhaps you wonder, *Can a big God really care about my daily particulars?* After all, "God is in heaven and you are on earth," goes the proverb, "so let your words be few."[4] While God inhabits realms far beyond our comprehension, I like to remember that he abides as close as our breath. Jesus reminded us that God numbers the hairs on our heads. God is relentlessly, extravagantly concerned about the puny details. Rather than frowning on our needy requests, he often delights in answering them with corresponding concreteness. He does not despise our urgent coming.

Kissing my wife good-bye in the morning, standing at the sink washing dishes, sitting at my desk trying to concentrate on my writing—there is no event or situation so common-place that God cannot be invited in. I can bring these and a thousand other grains from my life into my conversation with God.

Recently I had a bad day. I was leading a marathon board meeting at my office. Deadlines had left me scrambling to pull together the meeting's agenda until the last second. I felt flustered going in. To top it off, I had somehow managed to come without my own copy of a proposal I needed in order to lead the discussion. While I was very publicly reaching across the conference table to borrow a copy from a colleague, I knocked over a cup, spilling coffee and making a mess. Even now that clumsy moment captures and symbolizes a day I would rather forget.

The next morning, as I sat in my living room praying, I opened to the Psalms. My eyes fell on Psalm 20: "May the Lord answer you when you are in distress; may the God of Jacob protect you. . . . May he give you the desire of your heart and make all your plans succeed." I began praying that God would show tender care to my bruised ego.

I felt no great ecstasies, but prayer suddenly became keenly relevant. My performance at a committee meeting may not seem like much when wars loom or people die of AIDS, but every corner and crevice of our lives—even the gritty, sometimes-not-so-pleasant details—provide material for prayer.

But prayers born of need not only come naturally, they also teach us something profound about our relationship to God.

Prayer for Daily Matters Teaches Us That We Do Not Live by Ourselves, but in Dependence on God

Some of the holiest people I know realize that they are not the captains of their own souls. They know their expertise is not sufficient for all that life brings. For many of them that lesson came when a business venture came crashing down, a longed-for baby miscarried, a father died. They came to the place of saying, "I need resources inside that come from the outside."

Prayer born of need teaches us that humble dependence. God may even allow us to meet times of profound need because he knows that they have the potential to turn us toward him. In difficult times we are less likely to believe the myth that our ingenuity, charisma, and self-sufficiency are adequate.

Such moments can also bring us profound insights about God's care. When need drives us beyond ourselves, we discover a gracious, kind God who waits to bless us. "Come to me, all you who are weary and burdened" is the invitation, "and I will give you rest" (Matthew 11:28). Our resources may not be adequate, but God's are. We can take our need to God and leave it in his hands.

I think of Debra Bredican, whose story is told by writer Joan Wester Anderson. As a single parent, Debra struggled to raise a small daughter in a one-bedroom apartment in suburban Chicago. To supplement her salary, she made health food dinners for friends. Her client base grew as satisfied customers spread the word about Debra's menus.

But Debra knew she needed to expand. She would need a second bedroom for an office, plus an apartment manager who would let her install a second refrigerator. Both seemed impossible goals. And she couldn't afford more than a $650 monthly rental—which really was too modest for the area she had in mind. So she did the only thing she could: She prayed. And that is when "divine coincidences" began to happen.

First she found an apartment in a perfect location. But the two-bedroom rents were too expensive. She kept looking—and praying—and occasionally checked back with the complex.

"You're in luck," the rental agent told her one day. "Because of renovations we're lowering rents on all two-bedroom units over the next six months."

"How much?"

"Six hundred and fifty-two dollars," the agent answered.

But what about the two refrigerators? The agent laughed. That was just about impossible, she said, but she would see what she could do.

Debra went home, almost afraid to hope. But the next day the agent phoned. "This is odd, Debra," she began. "Remember I told you we're in the middle of a huge remodeling job? Well, we ordered two hundred and twenty new refrigerators. Yesterday they delivered two hundred and twenty-one. It will be cheaper for us to put the extra in your apartment than to send it back."

Debra went forward—independence. And her business is working.[5]

Prayer That Begins in Need Often Grows into Something Deeper and More Profound

The anxiety that prompts us to turn to God may ease once we are in his presence. Because in prayer we meet a God of inexhaustible resources, our desperation may relax a bit. And we may find ourselves free to think about something more than our own need. Prayer widens the horizons of our view.

So we pray like mad for a child (all the more if it's *our* child) going into surgery. We pray to keep our job when it's threatened. We pray to pass an exam. But we also stay open, once in God's presence, to whatever he may do or show us.

A student named Michael Allen found this:

I remember when I was in [graduate school] my best friend accused me of some dark and desperate betrayal. I did not know what it was about. But I was angry. I was angry at this friend who had rejected me. And I went to the chapel to try to work it out. I knelt down and my prayer came out in a mass of feeling. I pleaded with God to avenge me, to destroy my friend.

And I thought of all the ways the God of Israel, the Lord of the armies, who visits the sins of the father on the children, could do this thing. I savored my own anger, and then it began to taste bad. And the anger began to subside. Something else was welling up inside of me. And the something else was hurt, my own desperate hurt that my friend had rejected me, that I had lost someone I loved. And then I wept and asked the Lord to give me back my friend.[6]

Such insight becomes clear only when we sit in God's presence with our swirling feelings and poured-out cries. If we hold back in fear that we are not pure enough, we may never work through to the other side. "What we thought was simply blind desire," write psychologist-theologians Ann and Barry Ulanov, "starting out on its own, with nowhere in particular to go, turns out to be instead desire expressing a dim awareness of something already there. . . . But we do not discover this if we suppress or skip over our desires."[7] If God wants to take our needy prayers and shape and transform them, he can. We can speak urgently, and let him temper our excesses if he thinks he should. But in the meantime we need not worry. We can come to him, neediness and all.

The fear I felt in my Friday-night encounter with my bellowing downstairs neighbor turned out not to be the last word.

That Sunday my family and I went to church. The pastor stood up at the beginning of the service and said, somewhat apologetically, "I don't normally do this, but I feel moved to say that this place is a *safe* place. Some of you come from dangerous situations. But here you are safe."

Pastor Lobs had no idea what had happened to us just two nights before. He had no way of knowing about our jangled nerves and anxious thoughts. And he could not guess how much that word would mean to a family still suffering the jitters.

Was it coincidence? I prefer to believe that God knew what we had just been through. He knew we needed him. Not only did he not mind our coming to him with our panicked prayers, he did us one better. He gave us a wonderfully timed word of encouragement. He met us in our need.

Prayers

Lord, I see that I am not enough in myself. I think I can go along without giving you a thought. But then I stumble. Or I grow afraid. Or someone pains me.

Then I remember you. Be close to me in my need. And help me to love you even when no worry knocks on my door. Amen.

God our Father who urges us to pray, who makes it possible for us to pray, our plea is made to you, for when we pray to you, we live better and we are better.

Hear me groping in these glooms, and stretch out your right
hand to me. Shed your light on me, call me back from my wanderings. Bring yourself to me so that I may in the same way
return to you.

—AUGUSTINE[0]

2

The Simplest Language in the World

To God we use the simplest, shortest words we can find because eloquence is only air and noise to him.

—FREDERICK WILLIAM ROBERTSON

Your Father knows what you need before you ask him.

—JESUS

Crying to God is not done with the physical voice, but with the heart. . . . If, then, you cry to God, cry out inwardly where he hears you.

—AUGUSTINE

When my youngest son was two years old, chronic ear infections filled his ears with fluid, dulled his hearing, and slowed his mastery of speech. Micah wanted to talk, but a lack of words constantly frustrated his attempts. This made his part in our family's nightly bedside prayers a genuine trial. Especially when he took his turn after his highly verbal five-year-old brother, who managed, it seemed, to include in his prayers every neighbor and cousin he ever knew.

But Micah so yearned to participate that he bowed his head and prayed in what can be described only as an unrolling string of wordlike sounds and syllables. His praying had all the rhythm and inflection of real language. In the dark of the boys' room, his solemn efforts left us all alternating between stifled laughter and awe.

Not long after witnessing Micah's mumbled praying, our family moved to a suburb of Houston to gather a new congregation and build a new church. Sent off with the good wishes of friends and family, confident of our gifts and pastoral training, my wife and I went with high hopes. But almost as soon as we arrived, boomtown Houston went bust. The city's oil-industry economy dried up. People in our church moved away in search of jobs. After a year we realized that our fledgling venture was not going to meet expectations—not ours, not those of our financial backers. My wife and I slogged through two more years before we gave up.

During that difficult time I would sometimes awaken in the mornings with a dull emotional ache. I prayed often, and my prayer times became more frequent. But sometimes the best I could bring to my morning prayer times was a groaning spirit. No elegant, high-flying prose. No eminently quotable lines. Just heartfelt reaching out for comfort I could not smoothly articulate.

For all my adult ease with language, I am sometimes like Micah when praying. So, perhaps, are you. Words do not always come easily for the complex emotions that swirl within. Or, in the presence of unfathomable majesty, we wonder, *What can I say?* Or we think, *If God knows half of what he's supposed to know about me, how can I help being intimidated?* "I want to pray," I hear people say, "but I'm afraid I won't find the right words." Like the writer's terror of a blank page waiting to be filled with words, the prospect of addressing God can make us freeze up. We get "pray-er's block." We stutter through, afraid that God may not stand around waiting for us to "get it out." We worry so much about our words that our approach to God falters.

What can we do when words make us stumble?

To begin with, I try to remember that words do not matter as much as many suppose. They carry less weight than we think.

Our culture seems infatuated with words. By the millions they stream from our radios, TVs, newspapers, Internet sites, and books. Drive through any metropolitan area, with its billboards, neon ads, and bannered signs, and you get the strange sensation of driving through a huge dictionary or phone book. Words seem desperately essential to our lives.

But much that is profound can happen in their absence. "Your thoughts don't have words every day," wrote the stunningly articulate Emily Dickinson.[1] And when it comes to prayer, our spiritual impulses don't always need words either. What lies deepest within us may not need dazzling utterance. We may pray most profoundly when we actually say little. And pray most tritely when we say much. "The best prayers," wrote the seventeenth-century writer John Bunyan, "often have more groans than words." Stumbling at the words need not make any of us feel like second-class pray-ers. For all their roughness, both my praying and Micah's plumbed depths that polished phrases can never touch. Micah made up in sincerity what he lacked in fluency. And I now recognize my dark time in Texas as a time of growing intimacy with God.

In prayer, as in so many enterprises, we do well to make our words not the goal but the means. And when words cease being ends in themselves, we can relax with them. We stop being like the anxious teenager on his first date, trying so hard to be the wily, witty conversationalist that his partner can tell he's straining. Instead we just talk with God. "We don't need to use high-sounding words or try to structure our sentences to impress anybody," one woman explained. "I like to think of the Lord as sitting in a chair near me and I am conversing with Him."[2] This simple approach can free us in prayer to focus on relationship, not form. Words become a tool, not the work itself. We approach them as a wire or switch or other electrical conductor. We realize they play a vital part, but are not themselves the power that drives the motor or lights the filament. Words do not by themselves make prayer "happen."

While most of us would quickly define prayer as something expressed in words, I see it more fundamentally as our being in God's presence. Sometimes words are eminently appropriate. But sometimes they get in the way. And often they simply don't matter. The important thing is to stand before God without our constant chatter, ready to be in heartfelt relationship to him. Where our whole selves are engaged in relationship with God, there prayer will be, even if words are not used.

I also believe that our longing to pray itself can help us get through our difficulty. Our wanting is a great ally. We move ahead when we attend to our *desire* to pray. For the desire that propels us is ultimately a quest for intimacy with God, for a relationship that will go beyond words.

Linguists (and any parent) will tell you that babies seem to have an innate drive to talk. They don't need vocabulary drills and other techniques of formal training to learn. They begin to pick up words without prodding or pushing. The urge to talk, like the urge to walk, seems built into our genes. A child *wants* to squall out his or her need for milk, or giggle with affectionate patter, or call out for Daddy. We so long to relate to others, to express what is within, to hear what is within others, that language "happens."

So also is prayer something we want to do. In one sense nothing is more natural than praying. Once, I read that learning to pray is like mastering a foreign language. But that analogy breaks down. Because we are created to relate to

God, prayer is not foreign to our hearts. It is instinctive. Spending time with God does not usually require herculean effort, if only we pay attention to our truest desires, placed there by a Creator who makes us restless until we find our rest in him.

Psychiatrist Gerald May explains this through a story. Once he asked a young woman what she most deeply wanted. She responded immediately with typical concerns: a happy home and family, security, a sense of being worthwhile. Then May asked her to sit in silence for a moment and try to be open to what desires she could really *feel*. After a while he said, "she looked up with tears in her eyes. '. . . What I actually feel is that things are really okay right now. Better than okay. I don't think I want anything more than what I have at this very moment.' I asked her to be still once again, to look more deeply into her present feeling, to seek any desire that might honestly be there. Softly, she said, '. . . I want to say thank you to someone. Is it God? If it is, I want to . . . say thanks.' "[3]

The urge to turn to God is part of who we are, if only we listen long enough.

This means that when we do pray, often the most profound prayer is the simplest, because it arises from deep within, from some primal part of us whence comes not only words, but also memories, hurts, hopes, and all that makes us who we are. You don't need to be an expert in theological terms to speak to God. You need simply to be yourself. Prayer is the simplest language in the world. Micah discovered that.

Indeed the prayers of the great figures of the Bible display a disarming simplicity. Moses stammered his way through the times he had to address the people of Israel. "O Lord," he complained, "I have never been eloquent, neither in the past nor since you have spoken to your servant. I am slow of speech and tongue" (Exodus 4:10). And yet we read later that before God he conversed freely, "face to face" (Exodus 33:11). Prayer need not be eloquent to be real; it only needs to be from our true selves.

"Often," said John Climacus, a seventh-century Byzantine church leader, "it is the simple, repetitious phrases of a little child that our Father in heaven finds most irresistible." Thus prayer may employ the most elementary speech, the most natural expression.

I am startled to see spiritual giants, who could wax eloquent in prayer if anyone could, stress the same thing. The fourth-century monk Abba Macarius, for example, was asked, "How should one pray?" The elderly man said, "There is no need at all to make long discourses; it is enough to stretch out one's hand and say, 'Lord, as you will, and as you know, have mercy.' And if the conflict grows fiercer, say: 'Lord, help.' He knows very well what we need and shows us mercy."[4] What could be simpler? "Help!" is prayer in fine form, jangled exclamation and all.

Or here is the nineteenth-century saint Thérèse of Lisieux, who wrote of the folly of feeling like she needed some "formula of words" to pray: "I just do what children have to do before they learn to read. I tell God what I want quite simply, without any splendid turns of phrase, and somehow He always manages to understand me."[5]

Some of my best praying, I suspect, is done off the cuff and on the run—literally. I pray when I jog. I also pray when I drive to work, when I wait in line somewhere, when I drift off to sleep. Prayer at these times is possible because the whole tenor can be informal, unrehearsed. We can do "quick tales." We can cry out from the heart of our lives. You do not need to be in a pulpit or sanctuary; you do not need to have a prayer book open in front of you. You do not need thees and thous. What is in your heart can be in your prayers.

While God is awe-inspiring and almighty, prayer can still take on the qualities of daily conversation. We can converse as with a friend, with a lack of self-consciousness.

When words don't come, it helps me to remember another thing: *God does not stand far off as I struggle to speak.* He cares enough to listen with more than casual attention. He "translates" my scrubby words and hears what is truly inside. He hears my sighs and uncertain gropings as fine prose. We do not like to stand speechless or stammering before God, but that does not mean God holds it against us when we do.

I remember a vacation in France with my parents when I was in high school. I had just had two years of French, enough to learn the bare rudiments, but hardly enough to make me fluent. But there we were, tourists wanting to make everything of our time. So when we needed a bathroom, when we wanted to find a café, or when I lost my eyeglasses on the steps of L'Église du Sacré-Coeur and approached a policeman for help, I falteringly used my butchered French. I was trying—to the laughter of others, I suppose—to speak the language. But I remember more than the townspeople's bemusement: They warmly received my trying. They strained to hear past my fractured sentences and hopeless American accent. They honored me by responding. Is God any less generous?

According to a Jewish tradition, King David asked God to "understand what is in my heart."[6] Another Jewish tradition has it that God hears the faintest whisper.[7] "Before a word is on my tongue," says the psalm, "you know it completely, O Lord" (Psalm 139:4). That is a wonderful picture.

God bends his ear to all that arises from us—the words of our mouths, the longings of our heart, the thoughts of our minds, the intentions of our wills. Regret, grief, thanksgiving, hope—God hears our emotions, not just our grammar. Because of his grace, not our eloquence, we can pray. Even if we stammer and stutter.

I take heart in one more reality: *God helps me form even the words*. God joins his own powerful presence to what I try to say and do. A someone beyond my words comes and fills them out. "In the same way," writes Paul the apostle, "the Spirit helps us in our weakness. We do not know what we ought to pray for, but the Spirit himself intercedes with us with groans that words cannot express" (Romans 8:26).

There were times in those trying days in Texas when emotional energy failed to well up in abundance. When my words were few and my spirit tired, I had to depend on resources that went deeper than my own. I let God pray "through me." I would simply open my heart and my mind in the presence of God. I did not try hard to say much. Sometimes I found it helpful to *pray about my praying*. I asked God to help me find the words, carve out the time, find the motivation.

Prayer is ultimately something I participate in, not manufacture. I cooperate, not force. I am not suggesting passively letting God take over. We do not become subsumed into some cosmic oversoul that diminishes our individuality. But there are times when the Spirit helps us in a way that even surpasses our expectation. In the midst of our frustrated efforts suddenly there is an ease, a flow, a sense that we are not only praying but in some sense being prayed through.

Think of times you do something you truly enjoy. Immersed in your teaching or writing or painting, you become unaware of yourself, lost in the work of creation at hand. You become not so much an originator as a conduit. An energy seemingly not your own courses through you. You are more than your little efforts. You lose track of time, and straining ceases. That happens to me sometimes when I pray. The words stop mattering. They don't get in the way. Something—someone—carries them along.

One February afternoon some years ago, this happened to me in a memorable way. For months, really years, I had been praying for a breakthrough in my prayer life. I had been longing for a new fluency. That afternoon as I got back into my car after visiting someone in the hospital, I prayed about my praying. From within my soul, it seemed, streamed an intensity of praise to God and a longing not bound by words. Syllables formed new combinations beyond my conscious formulations or comprehension, carried along, it seemed, by the inward exuberance. Some call it "speaking in tongues." Others would say it was a kind of primal speech arising from some subterranean depths. All I know is that careful words seemed inadequate for the depth of my prayers, and God supplied what was lacking. When Paul the apostle contrasts "praying with my mind" and "praying in the Spirit" in the New Testament, I think that is at least partly what he had in mind. The Spirit can lift our praying beyond words, carrying our hearts to a communion and wonder that language cannot capture.

However it may happen for you, if you are growing in prayer, you will discover a deepening awareness of the divine side of the praying proposition. You will care less about articulating everything just so, and more and more open yourself to the one who first comes close to us in grace and continues to help us through his presence.

It has been a decade since my son graced our family's evening prayers with his holy jabbering, a decade since I learned to pray through my inarticulate groans. Micah has learned to talk like any typical thirteen-year-old. He gives his older brother a run for his money during our family's nightly prayer routine. But I still detect in him an occasional hesitation at piecing together the words. And I still have moments when my words (or lack of them) haven't caught up with the thoughts I want to express.

But I worry about that less than ever. I know that God hears Micah's praying as a wonderful offering of honest effort. And I believe God prefers my prayers from the gut over any verbal finery. Our desire to pray better is a sign that God has placed within us a desire not only to speak but to pray. Our imperfect words are prompted by God and heard by him. That realization can free us to come to prayer, however fine or fumbling our words.

Prayers

Lord, I do not know what to ask of you; only you know what I need. I simply present myself to you; I open my heart to you. I have no other desire than to accomplish your will. Teach me to pray. Amen.

—FRANÇOIS FÉNELON

Lord, help me not to worry about the words, but address you with the language of the heart, that my prayers, while not eloquent, will be sincere. Amen.

3

A Quietness of Soul

Eloquent silence is often better than eloquent speech.

—*JEWISH PROVERB*

Silence like a poultice, comes
To heal the blows of sound.

—*OLIVER WENDELL HOLMES*

In quietness and confidence is my strength.

—*ISAIAH 30:15*

I probably like "peace and quiet" as much as anybody. But I've noticed that in my commute to work, in what could be an oasis of quiet amid life's noise and rush, I often click on the car radio. And at home after a day of ringing phones and wordy meetings, I turn to television or crank up my CD player. Or I think of something needing to be done—a call to make, a garbage pail to empty. I rarely just sit in silence. I sometimes use sound and activity to avoid being alone with my thoughts.

A woman with a similar experience once told me, "I was cross-country skiing in the Canadian Rockies. A group of us spent the day climbing high, until we could see for miles the river basin and other peaks. We stood together, silent, atop a long trail we'd made through the snow. The only sounds were wind, an occasional snowbird, and the muffled noises of our beating hearts and breathing." But my friend remembers becoming uneasy. The calm was inspiring, but also unsettling. "We moved on pretty quickly," she said, "with a mixture of awe and discomfort."

Sometimes we seem to need the soothing constancy of sound or the numbing comfort of busyness. Have you ever found yourself growing itchy and restless when you are with someone and the conversation lags? Driving in a car with someone you don't know well, the silence becomes a hollow weight. You feel an obligation to fill it with animated conversation. No wonder we gauge the success of a social evening by the energy and volume of talk. We rarely see quiet and lack of activity as an occasion for communion with another.

Or we rush around. Our lists of tasks become tyrants. "For too long," writes Richard Foster, "we have been in a far country: a country of noise and hurry and crowds, a country of climb and push and shove, a country of frustration and fear and intimidation."[1]

It's not that we don't want moments of deep, satisfying quiet. Writer Eudora Welty tells of a time she spent sailing with the renowned novelist William Faulkner. "I was so happy he invited me," she remembers. "I don't think either of us spoke. That's all right. It was kind of magical to me. I was in the [man's] presence."[2] We have all had such moments enough to know they can enrich us. But quiet moments of refreshment are rare. And when we get them, our feelings are mixed. Our comfort level is fickle.

And even when we are alone—as we walk along a secluded wooded path, kneel alone in a chapel, or just sit on a front porch—powerful inner voices clamor for attention. The day's undone jobs cry out. Anxieties will not let us rest. There is little stillness within or around.

How frequently this happens when we pause for prayer! We want to spend time with God, but feel distracted by rush, wordiness, and emotional clutter. Prayer becomes a project, an exertion. We long for something more satisfying. We want to come to God with more than a ruffled, uncollected spirit. We want to go beyond constant chatter. So we wonder, *Is there a way through the noise? How do we silence the clamoring voices within?*

One of the simplest and most profound things we can do when we talk to God is simply to sit still. Many people begin prayer with the idea that they have to say or do something—

anything. I know I often come at God needing to make things happen. I think I have to get things rolling. I want answers.

But God usually intends for me to find rest or replenishment. Or simply to pause and *be*. I don't have to "perform" or achieve. I once heard my friend Steve Brown say that he does his best praying when he *stops* praying, when he finally ceases his gabby monologue and simply waits in God's presence.

Here is how Mark Galli, another friend, describes his discovery:

One warm summer night I lay awake, restless and lonely for my wife and children, who were away. Rather than picking up a book or watching late-night TV, my usual lines of defense, I went outside and lay on our lawn. I started to pray but decided instead to pay attention to what was going on around me.

I decided to look up. I spend most of my day focused at my level and below. At the office I see doors and windows and people and cars and the bottom half of buildings. But that night I consciously tilted my head. I saw the branches of our maple tree swaying against a sky dotted with a thousand stars.

I decided to listen. I spend most of my day in my head, listening to my own agenda whirl away, or at best, hearing the words of others. Now I listened to the wind, the rustling leaves.

I decided to feel, which I rarely have time to do. The warm air glided over my skin. Grass tickled my neck. Firm ground pressed against my back.

Suddenly, and for no more than a few seconds, I experienced mystery and beauty. I glimpsed the grandeur of the universe. I felt insignificant, yet love pulsed through me, around me. I became aware of the glory of God. I lay there, nearly in tears.

In prayer a gentle restfulness can steal over us. Our striving ceases. We sense a gentle, loving presence. "Often," writes my Internet friend Craig Petipren, "I just sit in awe of God in a very content state, much like a cat on the lap of its owner." Such a "prayer of quiet" produces a new openness in the soul, a letting go of our clamoring efforts. We find in prayer renewal, not just effort or strain. Such times in God's presence can bring a deep, abiding, soul-satisfying richness.

These moments may happen during an early-morning prayer time. While we walk from the parking lot to our office. As we sit in the family room with our children. As we click off the bedside lamp at night. They can even permeate the day's busy activity. Sometimes while engrossed in manuscript evaluation and author relations and contract negotiations, I find settling over me a calm, stilling presence. My soul shifts gears and becomes suddenly aware again of the Great Quiet of the God who permeates the universe. The stress and inner noise drop away.

How can we make more room for such an approach to prayer—and daily life? Learning quietness should not become another burdensome "project," of course. Communion with God depends on many things, not the least of which is God's choosing to show up and set us at ease; we need him to help us to gently receive what he brings. But it is also true that prayerful rest and calm do not happen by accident. Cultivating a quiet soul takes both patience and practice.

It should also be said that the purpose of quiet is not the mere absence of sound. It is not to eliminate thought but to make room for God's presence. The goal is to become more familiar with him. We often don't truly know people close to us (or even ourselves) because we rarely spend unrushed time with them. It is the same with God. We learn the art of not talking in order to hear what God wants to say. We practice "not doing" in order to allow God to do what God wants, which is usually far more than we can imagine. "Everything true and great grows in silence," wrote Ladislaus Boros.[3] When we cultivate a quietness of soul, God can find room in us to dwell and speak and guide.

What holds us back from cultivating quiet?

First, we live in noisy, harried times. In a TV-shaped world, a world dominated by blaring volume and video motion, calmness is seen as deadness. Our culture does not encourage it. "People haul their boom boxes to the seashore," notes philosopher Cornelius Plantinga, "so that they do not have to live in the silence between the rolling of surf and the crying of gulls, and so that no one else can live there either."[4] People who produce radio and movies and advertisements eagerly fill our silences. They compete, sometimes mercilessly, for our attention. Much conspires against our pondering anything in quiet.

A busy working wife, Kathryn, speaks for many of us: "I wish I always had time to go off alone and quiet myself. The fact of my life is that between a husband who doesn't really understand enough to encourage my private times and the hectic pace of a taxing job, it seldom happens."

Quiet is rarely handed to us. To find it requires going against the grain of habit and convention. We may need to remember that ensuring we get it won't necessarily be easy. Sometimes, when things are noisy at the house and I need to rush off to an errand, I stop myself. I grab my wife and we go for a quiet walk. Or I slow my frenzied rushing and decide to make the most of the time it takes me to get somewhere. That is not always much, but it is something.

Second, we will have to face ourselves in ways we like to avoid. All of us live with secret fears about ourselves. As long as my inner and outer worlds stay noisy and frenetic, I can ignore things I need to confront: my compromises, self-involvement, misgivings, lusts, guilt feelings, anxieties. When I am busy, when I don't listen to my deeper self, I can hide. When I am quiet, the beasts of greed or anger may rear up. It is not that they suddenly appear out of nowhere; they have lurked there all along. But as long as I talk or fill my mind with the talk of others, I feel safe.

But I miss an opportunity. For in silence I can confront

who I am, not in a threatening void but in the presence of a loving God. Where better to make painful discoveries than in the presence of One who can forgive us and remake us?

A friend suggested to John Edward Southall, a Quaker of several generations ago, that he should learn to be still in God's presence. This, he thought, would prove an easy matter. But no sooner had he begun

> than a perfect pandemonium of voices reached my ears, a thousand clamouring notes from without and within, until I could hear nothing but their noise and din. Never before did there seem so many things to be done, to be said, to be thought, and in every direction I was pushed and pulled and greeted with noisy acclamations of unspeakable unrest. It seemed necessary for me to listen to some of them, but God said, "Be still and know that I am God." As I listened and slowly learnt to obey and shut my ears to every sound, I found after a while that when the other voices ceased, or I ceased to hear them, there was a still small voice in the depths of my being that began to speak with an inexpressible tenderness, power, and comfort.[5]

In quiet moments God can help me meet my true "I," and lead me to a place of grace and new beginnings. So I need not ultimately fear what I will see or hear or find in silence.

Third, withdrawing from the press of activity seems like a waste of time, or at least a luxury. In a world of urgent need, of lonely senior citizens and abandoned crack babies, to sit and not *do* seems self-indulgent. "Retreating" to silence can seem like an escape from our responsibilities. I find I'm so used to deadlines at work, so accustomed to "efficiency," that I fidget mentally in the face of quiet. I bring a self-imposed urgency to everything I do. I am constantly aware of schedules and timetables. I rarely do things at a meditative pace. I hurry big for little reasons. But for most of us the greater temptations are not waste and escape, but talkativeness and incessant activity.

Times of quiet and withdrawal, we will find, can lead to greater profundity, more wisdom, increased effectiveness. When we stop to think about it, we realize how essential pulling back sometimes is. How much fresher we often are after a coffee break! Or consider an analogy: Music is beautiful not only for its notes but also for its pauses. You cannot have rhythm without the alternation of sound and silence. "There is a time for everything," said the writer of Ecclesiastes (3:1, 7), "a time to be silent and a time to speak." Even our daily breakfast conversations and work meetings and phone calls will have more depth and focus when we do not constantly hurry from one activity to the next. Creative withdrawal, occasional times apart to be quiet, can make all the difference. We need quiet to regain our sanity. We need it to pray.

One desert monk in the early centuries of Christianity used a wonderful picture: "When the door of the steambath," he said, "is continually left open, the heat inside rapidly escapes through it; likewise the soul, in its desire to say many things, dissipates its remembrance of God through the door of speech, even though everything it says may be good. . . . Timely silence, then, is precious, for it is nothing less than the mother of the wisest thoughts."[6] Reverential quiet, far from being a waste of time, can be a foundation for everything significant we do.

Fourth, being quiet means facing God. If we stop for a moment, we may actually hear or sense God. Perhaps we are not so sure we want to. What if God unsettles our preconceptions or prompts us to give up some things?

But facing God in silence offers the chance of a great encounter. His presence, his word, his call not only unsettle us, they also promise to change us for the better. "If we can pass through these initial fears and remain silent," spiritual writer Susan Muto explains, "we may experience a gradual waning of inner chaos. Silence becomes like a creative space in which we regain perspective on the whole."[7] We practice strategic withdrawal. We can gain a glimpse of God's wider horizons.

So you are sitting in a church service and it all seems like Sunday morning as usual. You are fighting boredom and wishing you had had more sleep. But then a sense of peaceful calm settles over you. You realize you are being *held.* Or you are praying, lying in bed, trying to shake off sleep and start a long day, trying to concentrate on just *being* with God, when all of a sudden you receive a gentle reminder that God is present, that he will accompany you through the day's events about to transpire. Or driving home in your car, nerves jangled while you think about the office and all the day's conversations, you are lifted above it all with a reassurance that allows you calmly to turn your attention to the people you are about to greet at home. Those gifts come wrapped in silence. They flourish in the loamy soil of attentive alertness. In the margins of quiet we learn to rest in God's presence.

How do we make space for restful silence? How do we overcome the seductive pull of words and sound and motion to heed God's invitation to "be still and know that I am God" (Psalm 46:10)?

I try to remember that much of my progress in prayer—whether in cultivating a quiet heart or in asking God for help—comes as a gift. We do not tame or manipulate God by any practice or discipline. The temptation is to reduce things to formulas and easily followed steps. But some things don't work that way. Cultivating a quiet heart is one.

I also try to remember that much of advance in prayer has to do with *waiting*. Waiting is not the same as being passive. It is not doing nothing. It is readying ourselves for something more. "Be still before the Lord and wait patiently for him," Psalm 37 tells us. Sometimes we need to say to ourselves, "Don't just do something; sit there." Our goal in prayer is not to make things happen on our timetable; it is to allow God to come to us. We cannot orchestrate his coming any more than we can force someone to love us. Gentle awareness of God comes as a mutual presence between two parties who come in loving expectation. My stillness in God's presence is a way to be ready.

"Saints listen for the sounds and silences of God," writes Cornelius Plantinga, "They quiet themselves into a kind of absorbency, a readiness to hear the word of God, and also the voice of God, and even some of the silences of God."[8] When God comes, I want my soul to be conditioned to respond, not with grasping but with gentle gratitude. I cannot do it on my own—I lack the discipline—but when I catch a glimmer of God, when he comes to dwell in my prayer times, I will want to turn toward him with what John of the Cross calls "a loving attention and a tranquil intellect." In such moments our souls will be awakened to an awareness that, while alert, is not agitated. "God is in his holy temple," wrote the Old Testament prophet when he saw God, "let all the earth be silent before him" (Habakkuk 2:20).

Silent awe before God is a gift, but it can be cultivated. We can learn attentiveness whether we spend our waking hours in an isolated office or a noisy house full of toddlers. I have found some practical things that help.

I have learned, for instance, to have *a set-apart time.* When I can, I awake early enough to get out of bed, go to the living room, and sit with my eyes closed for ten minutes. Setting a timer sometimes keeps me from looking at my watch every few minutes. I simply set it, and *wait.* I try to still the voices that rush at me, the tasks that need attention, the inner chatter that sometimes interferes with a focus on God. I try to turn the eyes of my heart to God with a simple, loving intention.

When my mind wanders, I repeat a single word or phrase that helps me regain my focus. Often I simply say the name *Jesus*. Or I gently say, over and over, *Lord*. This adoption of a sacred word to help focus praying is called by many "centering prayer." The idea is to gently supplant the distractions with a simple, habitual focus on a word. That can help lead my prayer out of my noisy inner world into its true center.

Classical writers on the spiritual life know that when we simply try to sit still in God's presence, especially at the beginning, our minds are out of practice. But when we use a simple sentence such as "O God, come to my assistance" or "Your will be done" or even just "Help me, God," it is easier to let the clamor of voices and thoughts pass by without being captivated by them.

"This way of simple prayer," writes Henri Nouwen,

when we are faithful to it and practice it at regular times, slowly leads us to an experience of rest and opens us to God's active presence. Moreover, we can take this prayer with us into a very busy day. When, for instance, we have spent twenty minutes sitting in the presence of God with the words "The Lord is my shepherd," they may slowly build a little nest for themselves in our heart and stay there for the rest of our busy day. Even while we are talking, studying, gardening, or building, the prayer can continue in our heart and keep us aware of God's ever-present guidance.[9]

Others use a prayer of Eastern Orthodox tradition known as the Jesus Prayer (made much of by a character in J. D. Salinger's novel *Franny and Zooey*). They repeat the phrase "Lord Jesus Christ, Son of the living God, have mercy on me, a sinner." Some use a string of beads to help them count the prayers. Often as I lie in bed in the morning, too drowsy to get up, too awake to sleep, this prayer beautifully helps my mind and heart turn to God. It helps me cut through the clutter and move from "self-consciousness to God-consciousness."[10]

My friend John Fafinski, a sales manager from Elgin, Illinois, describes his experience with the Jesus Prayer this way:

> I say the prayer in a slow, meditative way. I feel a sense of the nearness of God, that things that are weighing on my heart are being lifted up to God without my having to go verbally through the details. It's being in communion in a deep way that goes beyond words. If one of my kids is ill, instead of my having to name all the symptoms and say, "Lord, heal her," I just have a picture of her in my mind and I say, "Lord Jesus, have mercy." And it's as if I've lifted her up to the presence of Jesus. He knows far more about her condition than I could ever tell him.[11]

And while I believe the discipline of a quiet heart can and should be practiced whenever and wherever possible, I find that a set-apart time in the morning helps me to move through the day that follows with a greater awareness and inner calm. Starting with quietness helps me to continue to live with quietness.

It also helps to have a set-apart *place*. Some settings are more conducive to inner quiet than others. Sometimes a particular spot can possess hallowed associations for us. Our mind forms a habit of associating prayer with the feel of a certain place. That can help us enter naturally into a spirit of reverence. We can claim a corner of the living room or bedroom where we go simply to take refuge in prayer's restful quiet. I have not always found this easy, living in a house with three children, but it can be done. And when I arrive at my office in the morning, sometimes before many others have arrived, I sit for a moment, gaze out the window, and breathe in God's goodness. It helps me start my day on a note of calm and rest rather than frantic urgency. My office becomes a temporary sanctuary.

We can also adopt a set-apart *attitude*. During a break time we can pull our eyes away from the day's urgencies and remember to rest quietly in the Lord's presence. We can pause to draw back from the sound and fury. My friend Ann Denson tells of a particularly difficult time at an old job. "Sometimes it seemed all I could do just to keep my sanity." But she found that she could get through the day, even the most stressful, by breathing a prayer of barest simplicity: "I would simply repeat the name *Jesus*. It wasn't taking his name as a swear word, but as a prayer. And it made all the difference."

Consider "minute retreats" throughout your day. In the midst of pressing duties and a hectic pace, mentally withdraw. Take a deep breath. Put your feet up on your desk. And breathe quiet words of thanks to God.

Prayers

Lord, I am not good at slowing down. I like to see things "happen." I've become hurried and harried. And I like to fill the silences with sound.

Draw me to the rest I find in you. Remind me that time with you can re-create me and fill my life with all I need. Amen.

O Lord, the Scripture says "there is a time for silence and a time for speech." Savior, teach me the silence of humility, the silence of wisdom, the silence of love, the silence of perfection, the silence that speaks without words, the silence of faith.

Lord, teach me to silence my own heart that I may listen to the gentle movement of the Holy Spirit within me and sense the depths which are of God.

—FRANKFURT PRAYER (SIXTEENTH CENTURY)

O Lord, you know how busy I must be this day. If I forget you, please do not forget me.

—GENERAL LORD ASTLEY (ADAPTED)

4

The Way of
Intimacy

*God puts his ear so closely down to your lips that he can
hear your faintest whisper.*

—THOMAS DE WITT TALMADGE

A few years ago, as my mother was slowly losing her mind,
she unwittingly taught me something about prayer.

I had come from Illinois, where I lived at the time, to
visit her in her Santa Monica home, where I had grown up. I
knew from earlier visits that a series of strokes had been rob-
bing her strength and memory. But I did not realize what
that would mean for this visit.

"Do you know who I am?" I asked, leaning over the

steel rails of her bed, catching the attention of her vague, sunken eyes.

She shook her head no. She could not recognize me.

I placed before her eyes a framed picture of me as an infant I had just grabbed off her bedroom's maple dresser. In the picture I was chubby-cheeked, smiling.

"How cute!" she said.

"Do you know who it is?"

"No."

I knew she would never again recognize me as her son.

I made small talk then—the weather, my kids. But our conversation unsettled me. And in the years since, as her condition worsens, I have begun to see a pattern. The more meager her response, the harder I find it to talk—about anything. I love her and still try to make contact, but it takes more willpower to visit. I sometimes wonder how much my talking to her matters. And the loss of her loving attention makes me realize how much it has mattered all along.

Something similar can happen when we approach God. Nothing dampens enthusiasm for prayer like the fear of a feeble response. "For years," confessed one gospel music singer, "I wondered if my prayers *really* reached God's ears."[1] Do we get through? Someone once wrote me, "One of my greatest hindrances at the beginning of my spiritual journey was feeling silly and thinking that I was really talking to myself."

Worries like that nag at our attempts to pray more than most of us realize. They eat away at our conviction that praying even matters. Our uncertainties hang in the air—unspoken, perhaps barely thought—but they undermine our motivation. And when life gets hurried and harried, we drop whatever doesn't seem essential or fruitful. I look at my own schedule, for example, crammed with caring for my wife and three children, working at the office, writing a book in the evenings. Only believing that I will get in touch with Someone who notices and knows me will keep me at prayer. Without at least a glimmer of prayer's reality I would be hard-pressed to embrace a regular discipline.

I have read that when we are infants—as I was in the baby picture I showed my mother—an impulse to babble and gurgle arises automatically. But the jabbering won't *continue* automatically. It has to meet with response. In children with normal hearing—who are rewarded with feedback from parents—the babbling changes over time to become real language. But in deaf children, who are unable to hear the normal responses, the babbling trails off. Without intervention they simply stop "trying."[2]

With no expectation of response, our praying will likewise stop. Does God pay attention? Is God too far away to answer? Will we be heard? Prayer hinges on such questions. It has as much to do with the one who listens as with the one who speaks. For even more important than what we say is the character, the nature of the One who hears.

So with my experience with my mother still on my mind, I stand back from the words and sounds and think about the climate of prayer and my expectations.

Can I Expect God to Be Present—
Really Present?

Merely believing in the existence of God will not inspire much enthusiasm for prayer, and another analogy from life's intimate relationships shows why. Sitting in the same room only vaguely aware of your spouse or confidant or friend does not satisfy for long. When my wife, Jill, and I sit in the family room, weary and distracted at the end of a long day, sometimes one of us will say, "You don't seem very present to me." If I only occupy a chair, flipping through a newspaper while she talks, I will not inspire her to share deeply. She is not likely to feel much motivation to keep on talking.

When talking to God we likewise need to have more than a belief that God dwells "somewhere." We must know that he can be near and lend his ear. We want a very *present* God. Only the promise that I will be surrounded, held, and known makes prayer real.

I first realized that when I was on the threshold of adulthood. A seemingly chance campus conversation led me to the discovery that some great Someone was really there.

I was fourteen, full of the unfocused energies of adolescence, intrigued by the idealism and spiritual energy of California in the late 1960s. During lunch a classmate, Stan, joined me and my best friend, Don. The conversation soon turned to religion. Stan had become active in one of California's burgeoning churches, and he unblushingly talked about it. My friend Don wasn't so articulate. He was the son of a Polish Jew and a Mexican Catholic, and to no one's surprise—including his own—he was "searching."

But Stan was uninhibited in these matters. He asked Don, "Have you ever read the Bible?" I don't remember what Don said, but never will I forget the answer that began to form in me. It was as though someone had gently woken me up. I realized that years of church and Sunday school left me with little firsthand acquaintance with my faith, let alone the Bible. I certainly knew little about conversing with the God I paid lip service to.

I went home and began making my way—page by page—through the Bible. The stories about Jesus especially captivated me. And almost immediately I became aware of a *presence*. I had believed things *about* God, but now I began to sense—at times with a leap in my heart—that he was near—vividly so. I would awaken mornings and remember that right there, while still in bed, I could simply talk with God—have a conversation. I sensed that Jesus was somehow responsible for bringing him near.

Who knows what made that recognition come together at that time in my life? How can I explain it? All I know is that I became aware that I was not alone. God no longer hovered on the outer suburbs of my consciousness; he had moved to the center. And because for the first time I really believed someone was close, for the first time I prayed in more than the vaguest way.

Over the years that vivid sense of God's nearness has taken different forms, assumed varying levels of intensity or mellowness. But a conviction took root in me that has never really left me, and I have drawn on that innumerable times. Whether in everyday moments or in charged experiences of high worship, whether through snippets of prayer or intense crying out, I walk through life aware of a presence I can address. Sometimes the awareness comes dramatically, other times gently. The presence rarely overwhelms. But when we sense God is close, few things seem more natural than conversation with him.

The late Simone Weil, a profound chronicler of the spiritual life, at first kept herself at a distance from God. But she had developed a habit, whenever afflicted by her violent headaches, of saying the verses of George Herbert's poem "Love." At the time, she thought only that it was a beautiful poem that helped her keep her mind off her pain. But then something happened. She was caught off guard by a presence. "Without my knowing it," she wrote to a friend, "the recitation had the virtue of a prayer. It was during one of these recitations that . . . Christ himself came down and took possession of me." She continued, "I had never seen the possibility of . . . a real contact, person to person, here below, between a human being and God."[3] But then it happened. Prayer became possible.

In our day of sometimes vague spiritualities and fuzzy beliefs, I like to remember that relationships require another *person*. And so prayer requires a real God. Why work to learn the fine art of conversation and then neglect to find a friend to speak to? Who would take ballroom dancing classes but never expect to need a partner? The only reason prayer makes any sense at all is because there is someone to talk to who will care, and listen.

Perhaps more than we realize, we have all had moments of awareness of the unfathomable and ineffable that nudge us to speak and respond. We are mystics of the ordinary life. I may sense God's presence while out for a morning run, driving to my office, or simply waiting in line at a supermarket checkout aisle. We will sense him in a moment of profound stillness in a sanctuary, at a cresting of a hill on a mountain drive that takes our breath away, or during a dawning awareness that unseen arms uphold us during a harrowing chapter in our lives. The conviction will come that around me, above me, is Someone. I realize, *I am not alone*. And I pray.

Can We Expect God to Be Actively Involved?

As important as it is to say that Someone is really there, we still wonder what that "someone" is like. My image of God— loving or vindictive, attentive or absent, kind or callous— cannot help but affect my approach to him. What if God is there but does not care? What if he hears but is not moved? Is he truly personally involved?

I regularly teach about prayer, and in one of my sessions I assigned "homework": *During the week ahead, jot down in a notebook your mental pictures of God.*

When the class gathered next, a couple of people spoke of their perceptions of God as a kind of background presence— vaguely there, all right, but not necessarily an intimate presence. Not a God they could visualize as being vividly close.

One class member, however, told of a life-changing discovery. "For a long time," she confessed, "I pictured God as a colorless blob seated on a lofty throne—like at the Lincoln Memorial." It wasn't a threatening image, but neither was it very inspiring. Then one night, she told us, she had a dream. God appeared with the shape and substance and presence of a *person*. In her dream, God was no longer locked in his throne room. The being once vague and distant was out walking among the people, within the reach of her longing words. The change of image changed her whole approach to God. It made praying something to which she eagerly returned.

Another person told of growing up under a father who, while not physically abusive, was cutting and distant. "I think I'm afraid of God in ways I'm not aware of," she told us. Memories of her hurtful father shadow her praying still. Did she secretly fear that God might be like that? Would God be mean to her?

Here I find that logical arguments for God's existence alone will do little to motivate prayer. If the God to whom such reasoning points does not attract us, if God does not come across as actively kind, welcoming, and compassionate, our praying will lack passion. The awe-inspiring Cosmic Giant must also seem capable of being our friend. Otherwise we will hang back. Our interest will remain lukewarm.

It is no surprise, then, to find that the Bibles of Jewish and Christian tradition rarely resort to the cool, distant language of the philosopher when explaining prayer. The prophets and preachers and ordinary "everybodies" that populate the Bible's pages talk to and about God with names that come from relationships: shepherd, redeemer, husband, counselor. Their prayers have the simple but satisfying ring of conviction that someone who cares, who stays involved, is on the other side.

I also notice that time and again the biblical writers move from the impersonal third person *He* to a heartfelt second person *You.* They move from mere belief to prayer. From theology to devotion. And throughout history we see those who have walked the closest with God move from impersonal terms such as *The Almighty* or *the Lord God* to wonderfully comforting names, even terms of affection: *Loving God, Heavenly Father, Precious Lord, Breath of my breath, Hope from my youth.*

Ancient religious writers so sensed his caring that they pictured God as having not only a name but a *face.* The Lord used to speak to Moses "face to face," an old book of the Bible tells us. The psalmist longed for the "face of God." This is not to say in some woodenly literalistic way that God has bristly eyebrows and a white beard. It is to say that we experience God with immediacy and intimacy. God is majestic, but also accessible, loving. For Simone Weil, in the encounter described earlier, God became real, when, as she put it, "I . . . felt in the midst of my suffering the presence of a love, like that which one can read in the smile on a beloved face."[4]

The psychiatrist Robert Coles, in his landmark book *The Spiritual Lives of Children,* was moved to realize that of the children's 293 hand-drawn and colored pictures of God he has assigned and collected during his practice, all but

38 were of a *face*.[5] How else do we picture someone who not only exists but *cares*? God knows that whether we are young or old, rules, ideas, even ideals never satisfy our longings. Our yearnings end in a face.

That is why Christians make so much of Jesus: In him people meet a God who took on the contours and lines and gestures of human expression. Who assumed a human form to walk along the roads and dusty detours of human life. A God who incredibly, unbelievably, suffered to allow his own son to be hung on a cross in first-century Palestine to wash away forever the notion that anything could keep God far away. I need more than words, I have heard people say, I need a God with "skin." The God we sometimes picture as enshrouded in mist carries a name and shows a caring countenance.

How does this become more than mere proposition and head knowledge? Not through arduous philosophizing. Our questions about God are ultimately matters of relationship, not rationalism. They have more to do with our hearts than our heads.

A Pakistani woman named Bilquis Sheikh discovered this:

Suddenly, a breakthrough of hope flooded me. Suppose, just suppose God were like a father. If my earthly father would put aside everything to listen to me, wouldn't my heavenly Father . . . ?

Shaking with excitement, I got out of bed, sank to my knees on the rug, looked up to heaven and in rich new understanding called God "My Father."

I was not prepared for what happened. . . .

Hesitantly, I spoke his name aloud. I tried different ways of speaking to him. And then, as if something broke through for me I found myself trusting that he was indeed hearing me, just as my earthly father had always done.

"Father, O my Father God," I cried, with growing confidence. My voice seemed unusually loud in the large bedroom as I knelt on the rug beside my bed. But suddenly that room wasn't empty anymore. *He* was there! I could sense his presence. I could feel his hand laid gently on my head. It was as if I could *see* his eyes, filled with love and compassion. He was so close that I found myself laying my head on his knees like a little girl sitting at her father's feet. For a long time I knelt there, sobbing quietly, floating in his love. I found myself talking with him, apologizing for not having known him before. And again, came his loving compassion, like a warm blanket settling around me.[6]

The sentence humankind craves to hear, says novelist and essayist Reynolds Price, is "The Maker of all things loves and wants me."[7] That expresses our deep hope. I believe this is precisely why the Bible so often uses parental imagery for God. When Jesus' disciples asked how to pray, the first thing in Jesus' model prayer (known now as the Lord's Prayer) drew on the language of familial relationship: our Father.

Ah, but it is one thing for *Jesus* to address God with the

license of parent–child interaction. If anyone could, it would be *him*. But Jesus also taught that *we, too*, can use such a term of intimacy. "*Your* Father knows what you need before you ask him," he once told his audience of disciples and curious onlookers. And he told us to come to God in that very way, to address him as Father.

It is true that for some, abused and harassed by earthly fathers, the fatherly image does not evoke warm, nurturing memories. But the idea is to take the picture of an ideal father and blow that up large. For Jesus takes all that is good and rich in the image of human parenting and fathering and applies it to our relationship to God. At one point he even encourages us to call God *Abba*, an Aramaic term much like our *daddy*, akin to the child's first efforts to address his parent. Jesus is not suggesting sentimental childishness in our relationship with God, no, but trusting child*like*ness. He is unflinchingly insisting that we can address the same great Creator and Sustainer of all with the winsome intimacy of a child with its parents. Perhaps that is why wherever the New Testament speaks of requests being made to God, it emphasizes that God hears them. It emphasizes God's caring involvement.

When I was very small, perhaps four or five, I would often sit with my mother. She had an old, rock-hard maple rocking chair, and I would climb onto her lap while she held me and rocked me. Sometimes she sang children's ditties such as "Froggy Went a-Courtin'." I was held tight, safe. I could tell her when a bully was scaring me or a fall had bruised me. Sometimes I needed to ask something. Or just express my own child-like affection. At times like those I knew I had her attention.

That is how it always is in prayer. God does not forget us. Nothing impairs his hearing. It is this conviction—or even faltering hope—that allows us to pray. When we believe we are heard, we will pray. When we have even the faintest hope that someone responds, we will have the courage to keep praying. And nothing will hold us back. Whatever words I may reverently utter or simply fling his way, whatever struggle I sometimes have in sensing him, the reality that makes it all worth it is that God himself is listening.

Prayers

Lord, sometimes I wonder if you hear. But other times I am amazed at how quickly you listen and how surely you respond. You are like a kind, attentive parent! Help my trust in your relentless tenderness to grow. Amen.

Heavenly Father, you have promised to hear what we ask in the Name of your Son: Accept and fulfill our petitions, we pray, not as we ask in our ignorance, nor as we deserve in our sinfulness, but as you know and love us in your Son. . . . Amen.

—THE BOOK OF COMMON PRAYER

Part Two

What We Say

5

Facing Our Failings: When We Know We've Blown It

Our courteous Lord does not want his servants to despair even if they fall frequently and grievously. Our falling does not stop his loving us.

—JULIAN OF NORWICH

If the Spirit of God detects anything in your life that is wrong, He does not ask you to put it right; He asks you to accept the light, and He will put it right. A child of the light confesses instantly and stands bared before God; a child of the darkness says—Oh, I can explain that away.

—OSWALD CHAMBERS

The prayer preceding all prayers is "May it be the real I who speaks. May it be the real Thou that I speak to."

                    —C. S. LEWIS

During one year in college I met with a small group every week. From young adult singles to grandparents, engineers to housewives, we all wanted to grow spiritually. One evening we talked about admitting our faults to God through confession, but the discussion made someone I'll call Jeff fidgety. He finally blurted out, "I just don't understand all this. I'm a good person! I don't have anything to confess!"

I have never forgotten Jeff's puzzlement: He did not bilk senior citizens of life savings or push heroin. Why the need to pray about failings? To him the idea was foreign, even offensive.

But next consider someone I'll call Jennifer. When we talked, her husband had grown sullen and distant. Marital communication had ground to a standstill. As if the emotional barrenness at home were not enough, shame over her failing marriage kept her from turning to friends for comfort. Because she was about to give up on her marriage, and because her religious tradition frowned on divorce, she felt she was angering God. Guilt consumed her, so she stopped praying: "I feel unworthy, and it's driving me farther from God. I'm afraid that God won't hear my prayer." Far from feeling oblivious to guilt, she was paralyzed by it.

Between these two stories lies yet another: Michael is constantly trying to shake the nagging feeling that he doesn't "measure up." "I don't go to church enough," he sometimes says. "I spend too little time with my kids. And I don't call my mother as often as I should." Sometimes the pricks on his conscience comes from something more serious: failing to walk away when his law firm dabbles in illegal activities. Meeting a female colleague at a hotel over lunch hours. Guilt hounds his conscience. It does not debilitate him, but it certainly makes him miserable. It robs his life of joy.

However guilt affects us, in whichever story we see ourselves, confession forms a significant part of prayer. Just as we sometimes feel great relief when we can go to a friend and bare the things that distress our souls, just as we can all remember the joy of no longer having to hide some painful secret, confession to God can unfetter our praying. Indeed, without it, unresolved guilt may nag at our relating to God. Our prayers will seem troubled, anxious, uncertain. We will sense that something stands between us and intimacy with him.

And confession is more than a mere "outlet" for unsettled feelings, more than mere catharsis. Confession invites God into our failings and our littleness. It opens us to his forgiveness and empowerment for a different way of living. It is where our troubled consciences and God's love meet. And because confession ultimately involves both our feelings and God's response, several important things happen in and through it.

Sometimes Confession Is as Simple as Admitting Before God That Our Bloated Pride and Self-Involvement Do Not Fit Reality

On occasion we need to see our proper place. A psychiatrist, the joke goes, tells a client, "No, you don't have an inferiority complex. You really are inferior." Well, we *are* less than God. We will never run the risk of eclipsing him. We won't qualify as God impersonators. Humankind, the crown of God's creation, is prone to limits and foibles. Admitting that is usually good for the soul.

In fact in the presence of God's unfathomable greatness, it takes effort (or a huge ego) to avoid feeling small and incomplete. We inhabit a cosmos, I'm told, where a dime held at arm's length before the night sky would block fifteen million stars from view, should our eyes see with that power. The sheer vastness of the universe does not let us swagger long in self-importance.

No wonder the psalm writer, scratching his head in wonderment, penned,

> When I consider your heavens,
>> the work of your fingers,
> the moon and the stars,
>> which you have set in place,
> what is man that you are mindful of him?
>> (Psalm 8:3–4)

When we confess our smallness to God, we are simply reaffirming what reality would tell us daily, if we had a proper view. And if you or I recognize that we are a speck under the unimaginably deep canopy of the starry heavens, that one life is a blip in the grand sweep of world history, then the burden of having to "do it all" lifts. There is freedom in acknowledging our place. We see that we are not the only ones that matter, and the million things screaming for our attention, the mounds of tasks that make us feel indispensable, may suddenly lose some of their power. As we get a proper perspective, we relax a little. Confessing our smallness puts life—and our pride—in perspective.

So when I wander under a night sky, relax on a shore before an ocean panorama, or just sit in a room to pray, I see glimmers of the Great One who inhabits eternity. This helps me pray with appropriate humility. I find it easier not to think of myself more highly than I ought. And that glimpse of my place only magnifies God's amazing willingness to notice me, smallness and all.

Confession Asks That We Recognize Our Incompleteness—and That Can Be a Little More Difficult

I live in a world of the well-fed, well-dressed, and well-presented. Like me, many are addicted to being liked. We bask in the praise of others. We prefer the illusion that all is well with our souls. But under my niceness lurks an inner world of envy and ambition and seething hurts. I have things I would like to hide.

A story from novelist Harry Crews's memoir, *A Child-hood*, reminds me of this in an especially powerful way. He was remembering his poor rural Georgia upbringing and the hours he spent with the Sears, Roebuck catalog:

> I first became fascinated with the Sears catalog because all the people in its pages were perfect. Nearly everybody I knew had something missing, a finger cut off, a toe split, an ear half-chewed away, an eye clouded with blindness from a glancing fence staple. And if they didn't have something missing, they were carrying scars from barbed wire, or knives, or fishhooks. But the people in the catalog had no such hurts. They were not only whole, had all their arms and legs and toes and eyes on their unscarred bodies, but they were also beautiful . . . and on their faces were looks of happiness, even joy, looks I never saw much of in the faces of the people around me.
>
> Young as I was, though, I had known for a long time that it was all a lie. I knew that under those fancy clothes there had to be scars, there had to be swellings and boils of one kind or another because there was no other way to live in the world.[1]

For all its seeming appeal, protecting the veneer of right-ness robs life of liberating honesty. Our personal myths of near-perfection bring stiffness to relationships. We work so hard at looking good and smelling sweet that we rarely act natural or become truly transparent. We indulge in what political commentator Joe Klein calls "lawyering the truth."

When we try to hide our incompleteness from God, we make relating to him nearly impossible. Once I heard a friend say, "When I was growing up, I was always the 'good kid,' and I guess I bring the pressure from that into my relating to God. I find I often don't bring to God the gut-wrenching things going on in my life. I'm sometimes afraid to say, 'Lord, this is what I'm really like.' " But what freedom can come when we do!

One-time Nixon "hatchet man" Charles Colson learned this. In the wake of the Watergate scandal, he did some profound soul "inventorying." Then Colson visited a friend who tried to help him to face squarely what he had done. The friend referred to pride as being a kind of spiritual cancer that eats up the "very possibility of love or contentment." "Suddenly," Colson wrote, "I felt naked and unclean, my bravado defenses gone. I was exposed, unprotected. . . . [His words about pride] seemed to sum up what had happened to all of us at the White House. . . ." Colson couldn't shake the impact of his friend's tough words:

> Outside in the darkness, the iron grip I'd kept on my emotions began to relax. Tears welled up in my eyes as I groped in the darkness for the right key to start my car. . . .
>
> As I drove out of Tom's driveway, the tears were

flowing uncontrollably. There were no streetlights, no moonlight. The car headlights were flooding illumination before my eyes, but I was crying so hard it was like trying to swim underwater. I pulled to the side of the road not more than a hundred yards from the entrance to [my friend's] driveway. . . . I remember hoping that [my friend] wouldn't hear my sobbing, the only sound other than the chirping of crickets that penetrated the still of the night. With my face cupped in my hands, head learning forward against the wheel, I forgot about machismo, about pretenses, about fears of being weak. And as I did, I began to experience a wonderful feeling of being released. Then came the strange sensation that water was not only running down my cheeks, but surging through my whole body as well, cleansing and cooling as it went. They weren't tears of sadness and remorse, nor of joy—but somehow, tears of relief. And then I prayed my first real prayer.[2]

Confession is a way to slice through our defenses. It reminds us of our utter freedom to be incomplete before God. With God we can lay aside our shielding pride. When my perfectionism torments me, when I think I should be more and be able to do more, I turn to God in my disappointment. And I find comfort in admitting my limits before God. "I know what I am," we say in prayer. "I admit it: I do not have it all together."

More Than Anything Else, Confession Means Facing Hard into Our Moral Failings

Confession turns us back to God when we hurt others, transgress what is right, and follow what is false. Through confessing prayer we express our regret. We tell our piercing sorrow. We come, faults and all, not rationalizing or hiding or masking our wrongs. We admit not only that we sin but that we are sinners. That at the root of our lives we are "bent" away from God. We finally admit that we love the things of self and yawn in the awesome presence of God. We acknowledge that we obsess about our whims and recoil from self-sacrifice.

It is this dimension of confession that perhaps most goes against the grain of our culture. Moderns prefer a sunny view of human nature. Terms such as *sin* and *vice* have fallen out of fashion. You never hear them on the six o'clock news. But a stubborn refusal to face our moral brokenness creates constant pressure. It requires vigilance. So we "experiment," as Joe Klein suggests, feel vaguely guilty the morning after, but then protest too much about "how right" it felt. We shave corners and bend rules but prefer not to own up to our self-indulgent screwups. In office buildings across the country millions of people put up a Teflon exterior with the hope that when a project goes sour, no guilt will stick. Or marriages drift toward divorce when no one will admit to acting like a spoiled child. When we have to be right at all costs, in prayer or in daily life, our lives shrivel and shrink.

Just as bad, our stubborn refusal to be wrong drives us to

blame others—or anything. We become victims. We complain about the next guy. We feed a cycle of accusation and counteraccusation. We even blame impersonal forces. When we fail, says Edmund in Shakespeare's *King Lear*, even due to our own shortcomings, "we make guilty of our disasters the sun, the moon, and stars, as if we were villains [by] necessity . . . drunkards, liars, and adulterers by an enforced obedience of planetary influence."[3] We prefer to lay the onus on the stars or our genes or our parents. Anything to avoid seeing ourselves as flawed and anemic in virtue.

The words *good* and *evil*, notes a writer in *Newsweek*, "are often deemed too judgmental for public discourse. Even from pulpits, sin receives only mumbled acknowledgment."[4] But such categories help us name what we sense on a deep level to be true. Our guilt has a firm basis in reality. We are part of a fallen race. The theologians call it original sin. "All have sinned," the Scripture says, "and fall short of the glory of God" (Romans 3:23). Dig around in the compost of our psyches long enough and we cannot long avoid the moldering whiffs. We are not mistaken when we see sin in ourselves.

Of course I, too, am tempted to hedge when it comes to sin and evil. I tell myself that I do not indulge in the stuff of tabloid scandals. Like my friend Jeff, with whose story I began this chapter, I do not rob convenience stores. And while I battle the normal temptations of lust, greed, and callousness, my actual sins tend toward the respectable and subtle.

But when I am honest, I find plenty to fill my moments of confession.

One morning not long ago as I stood in my bathroom,

shaving and readying myself for the day, I realized with a wave of sadness how preoccupied I am with my own needs. Even my nobler projects—writing a book on prayer, teaching a Sunday-school class, raising a family—are twined with ambition and by my constant interest in *me*. Rarely do I ever rise above self. Daily relationships are marred by concern about how I compare with others. Even when I come to God, I'm thinking about what he can do for me.

My friend Kevin told me of a powerful prayer time he had recently. "Unusual for me, I spent most of my prayer time last Saturday confessing. It wasn't a maudlin affair. I simply realized how the whole of my life seems to center around work, around my success. The inner forces seem centripetal, throwing me inward, not centrifugal, throwing me outward to connect with others." Kevin did not mentally list his infractions; it was more like pondering what he *was* in the presence of God. It was seeing afresh the fundamental direction of his life while saying, "Yes, Lord, that's true what you are showing me." It was recognizing that without a front-end alignment he might end up in a ditch.

In our alienation from others, our lashing out at the innocent, our sensualism and gluttony (you name the sin), we need confession, which means, in its most literal definition, to agree with, to admit as true. When we confess, we agree with God that we are creatures prone to wander. We transgress his moral law and ignore our consciences, with inevitable consequences to ourselves and others. To understand the horrors that fill the headlines of our newspapers, to confront the dark impulses that drive and tempt us, we need more than a sociology textbook. We need God's reality check, even when it unsettles us.

Evil is not a dream. From the hideous crimes of a Pol Pot or Hitler, to the pesky meanness of a racist neighbor, to our own shadings of the truth, we cannot deny evil's reality. And we face it when we confess.

To unflinchingly face our sin is the beginning of our victory over its power to hold us back and keep us from God. "The man who knows his sins," said desert monk Isaac the Syrian centuries ago, "is greater than one who raises a dead man by his prayer."[5]

Facing our sins need not be a complicated affair. As you grow in your relationship with God, you will find him gently revealing things you need to acknowledge, seek forgiveness, and turn from. "Last week I said something flip and damaging about somebody I know," a friend recently told me. "Within twenty-four hours I had one of those 'ding' moments when, with the clarity of a bell ringing, I realized that what I had said was unfair." God has a way of pointing out our failings without our doing a lot of mournful probing.

So as you grow in prayer and sanctity, do not be surprised if your recourse to confession increases. For the more you rest in the presence of God, the more your imperfections may stand out. The nearer you stand to dazzling white, the harder it is to ignore the stains on your soul. It is no accident that when the prophet Isaiah had a vision of the Lord "seated on a throne," he immediately felt compelled to cry, "Woe is me! . . . I am a man of unclean lips and I live among a people of unclean lips, and my eyes have seen the King, the Lord Almighty" (Isaiah 6:1,5).

In Confessing We Find a Way
Through Guilt

On the other side of our coming clean with God lies not doleful dreariness but release and undreamed-of wholeness.

Confession may show us, first of all, that our guilt is not always true, not always centered on the right things. Most of us, I believe, have within us a sea of guilt. We are not always aware of it, but when we do something wrong—anything— the waves of remorse wash over us. Sometimes our guilt does not have a basis in fact. Some people I know are weighed down by an impossible system of *shoulds* and *should nots*. A woman may feel she should be a faultless cook and house- keeper, an always-available mother, a rising executive, and an effervescent companion for her husband—all at once. She is caught up in a cross fire of roles and cultural expectations no one person can hope to fulfill.

Or a man may unconsciously hark back to when he was a child trying to please a domineering parent. He secretly hopes that his careful compliance with the demands of his bosses will keep peace. When someone frowns or expresses annoy- ance, he frantically turns inward to find the fault that caused the breach. His oversensitive conscience does not lead him to God but to self-absorption. Guilt becomes a disease that ren- ders him a spiritual invalid. He hasn't done something wrong; he is experiencing what some call pseudoguilt.

Here confession can have a healing role. It frees us from the mire of self-recrimination so that we can breathe the fresh air of grace. Even the smallest trifle, if it makes us feel uncomfortable or guilty, should be brought into prayer. If it should turn out to be pseudoguilt, then our time in the healing presence of God will reveal that. The guilt will drop away. Each time of confession before God will serve to develop healthier patterns for our relating and reacting.

And when our guilt *is* appropriate (as it often is), confession turns us toward a God who has power to do something about it. The dis-ease we *should* feel when we do wrong drives us into the arms of God. Then our guilt does not rise between us and God as a wall, but as a bridge.

> When I kept silent,
>> my bones wasted away
>> through my groaning all day long.
> For day and night
>> your hand was heavy upon me;
> my strength was sapped
>> as in the heat of summer.
> Then I acknowledged my sin to you
>> and did not cover up my iniquity.
> I said, "I will confess
>> my transgressions to the Lord"—
> and you forgave
>> the guilt of my sin. (Psalms 32:3–5)

So it is true that sin separates us from God. Sin leaves us immersed in self and turned from him. But God overcomes its effects. Our feeling unworthy does not need to keep us from God. Instead it can open us to our need for God's mercy like nothing else. "This is love," we read in the Bible, "not that we loved God, but that he loved us and sent his Son as an atoning sacrificing for our sins" (1 John 4:10).

In some primal, mysterious way Jesus took into himself the world's evil and redeemed it on the cross. His blood became our peace, his broken body our hope. He reconciled us to God. He restored what had been shattered by guilt. "This is that mystery," said Martin Luther centuries ago, "which is rich in divine grace unto sinners: wherein by a wonderful exchange, our sins are no longer ours but Christ's; and the righteousness of Christ is not Christ's but ours. He has emptied himself of his righteousness that he might clothe us with it, and fill us with it; and he has taken our evils upon himself that he might deliver us from them."[6] God will not let our guilt stand between us and him if we are willing to let him wash it away.

Out of his graciousness God invites us to come, warts (and worse) and all. He does not demand perfection, only a "broken and contrite heart" (Psalm 51:17). Because of what he has done and told us in Jesus Christ, we do not shrink back or come with our guard up. We come humbly, but also knowing that we will not be laughed out of the throne room. We approach God with "freedom and confidence" (Ephesians 3:12).

We also come with hope. Confession does more than bring us closure with the past. It can lead us into the presence of a transforming power that can help us change and become more than we are. God can lift us out of our ruts of habit and inclination. He can inspire and strengthen us for new patterns, new choices.

When I feel guilty, I know to pray. I turn toward forgiveness. I see how grace, not my performance, is what matters. And that gives me great courage, even knowing I will sometimes falter, and even fail.

Prayers

Have mercy on me, O God,
  according to your unfailing love;
according to your great compassion
  blot out my transgressions.
Wash away all my iniquity
  and cleanse me from my sin.
For I know my transgressions,
  and my sin is ever before me.
Create in me a pure heart, O God,
  and renew a steadfast spirit within me.
Do not cast me from your presence
  or take your Holy Spirit from me.
Restore to me the joy of your salvation
  and grant me a willing spirit, to sustain me.

—PSALM 51:1–3; 10–12

Come, let us to the Lord our God
With contrite hearts return;
Our God is gracious, nor will leave
the desolate to mourn.

—JOHN MORISON (EIGHTEENTH CENTURY)[7]

6

Celebrating
God

*A single grateful thought raised to heaven is the most per-
fect prayer.*

—GOTTHOLD EPHRAIM LESSING

*Adoration is the lifting up of the heart and mind to God,
asking nothing but to enjoy God's presence.*

—THE BOOK OF COMMON PRAYER

Early one morning not long ago I sat down with a list of concerns and tried—earnestly—to pray. Toward the top of the
list was my ailing mother. My wife and kids, my brother and
his family. Farther down was the name of a friend who was
writing a book and needed all the wisdom and help he could

get. And how could I forget the war in Bosnia? Two dozen items called out for my attention. But something wasn't right. It could have been my sluggish, drowsy mind (it was, after all, five A.M.), or my distracted worrying over a project at work (which was what had awakened me in the first place). But more than anything, I think I simply needed prayer that morning to go beyond asking. Something in me wanted to rise above my prayer "agenda." I first had to silence my unquiet mind to give voice to something even deeper than need.

While our lives' daily needs may drive us to God, they can also clutter our praying. Our souls can become bothered with what a friend of mine calls "muchness and manyness." If *all* I do is ask, I may become only more agitated. Prayer becomes an urgent transaction rather than an encounter. A friend of mine once said, "I come to prayer like I do to a fast-food restaurant, instead of to elegant dining. And my spirit is becoming malnourished." The urgency and desire to see things "happen" that initially drove us to our knees can also drive us to distraction.

When prayer becomes as hurried and hassled as our nine-to-five lives, we cover ground, but rarely stand on holy ground. We pray for the things we want to see changed but then forget to pause and consider whom we are addressing. While I believe I should ask—earnestly and without guilt—I frequently find myself rediscovering another side to prayer that can be even more profound and life-changing. My spiritual sanity cannot do without time for pondering and enjoying God.

In this way I find myself lifted out of life's littleness. I become caught up in a vision of Someone who captures the attention of the most profound longings of my soul. One writer calls it the "cultivated habit of looking up and away from myself."[1] I come to God ready to enjoy God. I stand back from the striving and talking in order to remember the wonderful Reality whom I address.

What is the chief end of humankind? asks a venerable Scottish catechism. Schoolchildren for generations have learned the concise answer: "To glorify God and *enjoy* him forever." Significant things happen when we simply gaze in God's direction. Our desperately urgent agendas may wane, our concerns about our world paling next to the One who inhabits heaven. We learn simply to take pleasure in a great and wonderful God. "One day," my friend Marge told me, "I was praying. I heard a small, quiet, but very distinct sentence, 'Stop trying so hard.' I had trouble believing what I was being told, so I asked God, 'Then how do you want me to pray?' I don't remember whether I got an answer, but I *relaxed*. I started paying attention to *God*. Since then I have learned how important it is to allow myself simply to be in his presence."

Many are the times I can recall when on a morning run or at late-night prayer time I have simply meditated on God. At such times I think gently of his presence. I don't try to say much. Or do much. I simply rest in an unhurried awareness. Sometimes I conclude these prayer times with a vague uneasiness that I haven't brought to mind many requests. A number of important stones have gone unturned. But there steals over me an even stronger, more profound sense of being "done," of prayer having done its work.

The power of spending gentle, joyous time in God's presence comes from the recognition that he is great, that my soul will find much to feed on. We can be, as one writer suggests, "fascinated" with God. "We admire athletes for their strength and musicians for their talents. The abilities of the sculptor amaze us. The charisma of the statesman fascinates us. Yet we are so seldom fascinated with God. . . . Prayer is an excellent means of refreshing our appreciation of God."[2]

But there is more. We can add to our simple enjoyment of God awe and wonder.

We live in times, my former California pastor Donald Shelby likes to say, that are more characterized by "blah" than "ah!" So our souls may need practice in cultivating this attention to grandeur. We need our capacity for quiet amazement expanded, for we tend to project our jaded outlooks onto God. We think small and expect little. But he is bigger and better than our imaginations can conceive. In a universe rife with the unfathomable, awe is the soul's appropriate stance.

The glories of the natural world, for example, point to the glory of God. They help us think about the hand behind the handiwork, the miraculous power behind the marvel. One simple way to remember this is to sit quietly in a forest, or watch the clouds dance on a blustery fall day, or stand in the spray of a waterfall, or walk an urban street after new snowfall has scoured the city's grime with its gentle white. "The heavens declare the glory of God," said David of Israel. "The skies proclaim the work of his hands. Day after day they pour forth speech" (Psalm 19:1–2).

But for all the grandeur and dazzle of the universe's natural wonders, there is something even greater to inspire our awe. The crown of God's creation, humankind, is "fearfully and wonderfully made," as David put it (Psalm 139:14). The charged intimacy of romantic love, the heroic compassion of a saint, the simple pleasure of conversing with a friend all remind us of the goodness of God's creation in humankind. He saturates our human life with his creative genius. A sense of wonder is a natural response here as well.

When we see the wonders of earth and humankind, when we remember that he *made* us and controls creation still, we realize his glory all the more. The most awe-inspiring vista, the most breathtaking mountain scene, the most powerful natural force all point not to themselves but to a God who holds them easily in his hands:

> I know that the Lord is great,
>   that our Lord is greater than all gods.
> The Lord does whatever pleases him,
>   in the heavens and on the earth,
>   in the seas and in their depths.
> He makes clouds rise from the ends of the earth;
>   he sends lightning with the rain
>   and brings out the wind from his storehouses.
>   (Psalm 135:5–7)

As important as living with a sense of wonder is, this does not exhaust our celebration of God. We admire the heavens, the seas, the mountains, but nature cannot satisfy our longing to *express* our awe. Redwood forests and sunsets move us, but as objects of worshipful love they fail, no matter how breathtaking. A woman who had given up on religious faith was hiking amid the beauty of the Swiss Alps. She wrote to a friend, "I long to make some small sound of praise to someone, but whom?" We need some*one* to adore.

Wonder therefore gives way to another impulse of the praying heart: praise. We say not only, "What beauty!" but also "What a great God!" We do more than bask in the sunshine. "One's mind," as C. S. Lewis writes, "runs back up the sunbeam to the sun."[3] We give our wonder a name and we praise the source. When we come to God with adoration, it is not so much for what he has created as *who he is*. We worship and love him for himself. We honor and glorify him who existed from eternity.

The biblical record is replete with praise and adoration, as this example from the Psalms shows:

> I will exalt you, my god the King;
>> I will praise your name for ever and ever.
> Every day I will praise you
>> and extol your name for ever and ever.
> Great is the Lord and most worthy of praise;
>> his greatness no one can fathom. (Psalm 145:1–3)

In the Bible's New Testament alone the passages that urge or describe praise and thanksgiving number well over two hundred. The Bible's words take on astonishing variety: *bless, worship, glorify, magnify, extol,* to name just a few. They all point to the fact that as we see God for who God is, our response is rightly one of adoring worship.

Praise can be one constant in our praying, even as other aspects of our lives shake or crumble. Some years ago my wife went through a particularly dismal and discouraging time. She was feeling stung by criticism from a handful of the members of the church where we were on pastoral staff. She brought her hurt easily to her prayers. But then she began to cut through her pain by doing something that seemed almost irrational: She filled her praying with praise. Far from sensing she was living in denial, she felt more whole, more *herself,* more like she was doing what she was made to do. The goodness of God emerged to her as the true reality. Had her prayers only gathered her complaints, she would have missed a significant revelation.

No matter what happens to us in our daily lives, God stays the same. The Bible's depictions of God as good, trustworthy, sufficient, loving, mighty, steadfast, generous, able, merciful, truthful, and victorious are all sources of bedrock hope. Along with our anguished cries for help we can voice prayers saturated with certainties about God's immutable goodness.

This emphasis on praise, however, leaves in some people's minds a question. If God is God, why should he care whether we honor him with our praises? "When I first began to draw near to belief in God," writes C. S. Lewis, "I found a stumbling block in the demand so clamorously made by all religious people that we should 'praise' God; still more in the suggestion that God Himself demanded it. . . . It was hideously like saying, 'What I most want is to be told that I am great and good.' "[4] After all, we despise a man or woman who, in seeming insecurity, insists on being complimented.

But when we call a painting "admirable," reflected Lewis, what do we mean? That admiration is the correct or appropriate response. That if we praise such a work, it will not be senseless or out of touch with reality. Indeed, not to do so may indicate more about crude insensitivity than anything else. Praise, then, is not just a subjective whim; it is God's due. It is expected. It is right. And we fall short if we, curmudgeonlike, withhold it.

And because appreciation, love, delight all strive for an outlet or object, to keep our enjoyment in God's presence unarticulated or unnoticed diminishes us. Bottled up, the impulse to praise will grow faint. Unexpressed, it will not enrich our souls. It will languish, just as love for another person never expressed will always be a frustrated love. To praise that which is praiseworthy does something for us. And the more worthy the object, the more exalted our appreciation, the more intense our delight in expressing it.

———

Wonder and praise do not exhaust our repertoire for celebrating God. When we glory in who God is, we not only praise him for his immutable being, we thank him for particular blessings. But here again, we can use practice.

Whatever you make of the thesis of the recent book *The Culture of Complaint*, the title alone speaks volumes. It is more fashionable to grouse and pretend that nothing and no one can satisfy us. But a dulled, blasé outlook robs our praying of its power. I have a friend who recently concluded that his thinking and praying have been too much laced with discontent. Now he wants to replace his murmuring with an "attitude of gratitude." I know what he means. I find it easy to dwell in prayer on what I need, but neglect to mention with thankful breath what I have already received. I let daily pressures so consume my waking life that I forget the gentle joy of living thankfully.

Making thankfulness a fixture in our daily outlook is not always easy, of course. Some years ago my friends Jeff and Diane faced a tragedy. Within hours of giving birth to their first child, a doctor told them that tiny Joshua was "underdeveloped and retarded." Diane remembers the first night after the diagnosis: "It was a sleepless time, with the word *retarded* echoing all night. It seemed like a nightmare."

Jeff faced his struggle the next day. He had long before promised the Ohio congregation where he was a student pastor that he would drive out and let them know when the baby was born. He would get the word out, he had said, by ringing the church's steeple bell. "When I was wrestling with why this had happened to me," Jeff told me, "I thought, *I don't want to ring the bell*. After all, bells usually had to do with *good, joyful* news. What should I do in the midst of disappointment?"

After an early morning time of grief and wrestling prayer, Jeff knew what to do: "I got cleaned up and changed, ate breakfast, and headed for the church. I decided to ring the bell."

Hearing Jeff and Diane talk about Joshua, now a cherished young man of twenty, made me think of Paul the apostle's words in the New Testament to "give thanks in all circumstances" (1 Thessalonians 5:18). On the surface, such advice seems to run counter to all reason. But when we learn the fine art of living gratefully, we thank God even for life's sometimes hidden or disguised blessings. God gives us the ability to be grateful even when things are hard. We are able to ring steeple bells even in sadness.

Grief and inconvenience are not our only challenge to living and praying thankfully. Our daily routines can get us out of the habit of thankfulness. Sometimes I become amazed at how oblivious I've become to all that I have to be grateful for. Not long ago, my wife narrowly missed serious injury—potentially fatal—when the car's accelerator got stuck. When she told me afterward about her harrowing maneuvering through busy intersections—without mishap—I was filled with gratefulness that she was fine. But why wasn't I that thankful for her all along? A nasty software virus put my

computer out of commission for the better part of a week:
when I got it back from the shop, how grateful I was to sit
down and use it once again, and realize that almost none of
my files had been lost. Why wasn't I grateful before I almost
lost it all?

Simple distractions also war against a thankful attitude.
When you are barely holding on amid the stress of many
demands, it is not always easy to feel thankful. My friend
Marge has an antidote: "When I get distracted or I 'dry up'
spiritually, I simply sit in my 'prayer spot'—a chair in the
corner of my living room by a window. And if I'm having
trouble, I look out the window and start with prayers of
simple thanksgiving—for the diamonds of dew on the grass,
for the translucent pink of a baby rabbit's ear backlit by the
morning sun. I think, *This is all a gift*. Then I take it one step
farther, to think about my children, who are even greater
gifts to be grateful for."

I often find it helpful to block off prayer time for
nothing but thanks. I mentally list the things for which I am
grateful: a loving wife, children who are thriving, a house
that keeps us warm in winter and cool in summer, meals
enough to keep our bodies strong, work to do, friends who
care. Or as I go through the day, I try to have a mind of
thankfulness. One morning not long ago I decided to devote
the entire day to thanksgiving. As much as I could, whenever I prayed, I would not ask or seek or tell; I would only
thank. On the surface it was a normal day, but deep inside I
was rejoicing. I was celebrating God. As I write this
moment, the sunshine of a crisp October morning streams

into my bedroom through the window near my desk. As I not only enjoy it but thank someone for it, I find life infused with gratitude.

So it is not denial or flight from reality that has us thanking; it is recognition that life itself is a gift. That even the hardest times contain, if we but look, traces of a goodness worthy of a lifetime of gratefulness.

Every now and then I ask myself how I can offer up more wonder, praise, and thanksgiving; I would like not to live being so forgetful of God's goodness. Brother Lawrence, who penned the spiritual classic *The Practice of the Presence of God*, wrote of how he kept himself in a "simple attentiveness and a loving gaze upon God."[5] That's it! At first, as we try to live a life even faintly characterized by thankful praise, we will find it easy to fall back into old patterns. But we can learn new habits of enjoying God. We can fill our thoughts with promises of God's constancy and dependability. We can call to mind the many times he has shown his faithfulness in the hard times of our past. And we can immerse our praying in the praises of the Bible, the church's worship and music of faith, and the words of spiritual writers who have learned the language of adoring devotion. And we can allow a shaft of sunlight, a starry night, a child's loving gaze to point us toward the Maker and Sustainer.

Praise will grow in us as a response to the God at work within us and about us. A life of thankfulness and praise is not found through fierce mental concentration as much as through cultivating a loving heart. We allow ourselves to rest lovingly in God, and an outpoured offering to God will follow.

Might not life be different if enjoying God formed the backdrop of our praying and living? As we wash the dishes after supper, as we sit at our desk doing finances, as we wait with bated breath for a call from a wayward child, what if we filled our minds with words that flow from what we believe about a caring, wonderful God?

Prayers

Worthy of praise from every mouth,
of confession from every tongue,
of worship from every creature,
is your glorious name, O Father, Son, and Holy Spirit:
who created the world in your grace
and by your compassion saved the world.
To thy majesty, O God, ten thousand times ten thousand
bow down and adore, singing and praising without ceasing
*   and saying,*
Holy, holy, holy, Lord God of hosts;
Heaven and earth are full of your praises;
Hosanna in the highest.
—FROM A FIFTH-CENTURY NESTORIAN LITURGY (ADAPTED)

We worship you, O Lord God, and give thanks to you for your
great glory and power, which you show to your servants in

your wonderful world. All the things which we enjoy are from your mighty hand, and you alone are to be praised for all the blessings of the life that now is. Make us thankful to you for all your mercies and more ready to serve you with all our heart; for the sake of Jesus Christ. Amen.

—FROM THE NARROW WAY (1869)[6]

7

Not Being Afraid to Ask

A prayer in its simplest definition is merely a wish turned Godward.

—PHILLIPS BROOKS

More things are wrought by prayer than this world dreams of.

—ALFRED, LORD TENNYSON

Some people think God does not like to be troubled with our constant asking. The way to trouble God is not to come at all.

—DWIGHT L. MOODY

In my earliest memory from childhood I am knocking on a locked bedroom door. I must have been three or four years old. I stood outside my parents' bedroom, clamoring and calling to get in. On the door's other side my parents wanted some privacy. Everything in me focused on asking, on getting through. But there was a barrier between us.

It was that way again when I was twenty-two. I desperately wanted my parents to come to my wedding. But their fears, their unwillingness to let go, their own plans for me made them refuse. How I asked and asked them to come! Through heated, sometimes tearful arguments, through impassioned letters, I tried to persuade them. They did not relent. But I never stopped asking. Nor did I stop wanting their blessing once I was married. Phone calls, letters, and cards (and the advent of their first grandchild) eventually brought them back.

Throughout my forty-some years of life I have found myself often assuming the posture of knocking and asking. I do it differently now of course than I did as a toddler. I have learned some manners, and try to show an adult's patience. But in relationships, on the job, or doing much of anything that involves others, I cannot go for long without actively expressing my wants and hopes. Who of us can? In healthy relationships—especially intimate ones—we cannot stand passively by. Few things are more natural to us than asking.

"Prayer," a towering, white-haired, gravelly-voiced professor from my graduate school once said, "is a form of protest with

God against reality." That line slays the myth that spirituality makes us greet injustice or the status quo with a shrug. Folding our hands in prayer is not an act of resignation. Prayer does not lead us to accept every circumstance with passive calm. In fact a quarrel with our world as we know it can be a great ally in the spiritual life. A desire for change often *drives* us to prayer.

And because spirituality does not mean a retreat to indifference, asking—even the impetuous and noisy kind—holds a hallowed place in our talking to God. Sometimes we must pray for what can be. Or pray against what is.

Remember Tevye in *Fiddler on the Roof?* He wonders out loud if it would really "spoil some vast eternal plan" if God would make him a rich man. With that unaffected, unselfconscious whimsy comes a serious side. We live in a world of Bosnian killing fields, Alzheimer's disease, and molested innocents. Every day we see evidence that the things around us and the people next to us need help. No caring person can glibly, blithely assent to the world as it is. Nor do we need to. We can pray. We can ask.

It comes as a surprise to some to hear that the words for prayer in the original languages of the Bible literally mean "ask," "request," "beg," and "beseech." In the Old Testament we more than once hear a thundering "Why?" or "How long?" Prayer is an outlet for the nagging, restless feeling that tells us all is not right.

I see this in the New Testament as well. Jesus was frank and uncondemning in acknowledging that we will often come to God with urgent requests on our lips. "Ask . . ." he said with blunt imperatives, "seek . . . knock." He himself often came to God asking, begging God to keep his followers together, to give him guidance, and ultimately to keep him from facing a horrible death.

Jesus told a wonderfully odd story to make sure we don't give up on asking prayer. A woman, he said, a widow, kept nagging a crabby judge for "justice" against her adversary. She felt wronged, and would not stop pestering the judge until he ruled on her behalf. She was persistent to the point of rudeness. She had nerve. Why did the case come out in her favor? The official couldn't care less about God or widows. It was, Jesus said, so that the woman would not "eventually wear out" the poor man with her nagging. Think about it, then: If an irritable, insensitive judge will respond, how much more will God? So why worry about asking? Asking is not the *only* ingredient of prayer, but it is where most of us start. And it is the kind of praying the biblical greats most often unblushingly brought to God. They prayed for forgiveness for their sins, for success in their work, for many years of vigorous life. They filled their prayers with requests for their nation, for victory in war, for justice to win out, for people to turn to God, for God's kingdom to come.

On this basic, almost instinctual level, asking prayer makes wonderful sense. But think about it a little more, and it may not seem so simple.

My friend Randall sometimes wonders about coming to God with requests. "Say I am looking for my lost car keys," he said. "I may ask for God's help. But God from his throne sees where the keys are. He knows I'm looking for them. What sense does it make to ask?" Or, to put it another way, isn't it all terrifically redundant? We say that God knows all, that nothing is hidden from his sight. Yet much of our praying seems to consist of informing him of things. Or at least reminding him. Couldn't things be more spiritually "efficient"? We could let God simply read our minds. Or we could assume that whatever comes is God's best. Isn't anything else interfering with the plans of someone who already knows better than we what should happen?

A journalist friend of mine takes an even blunter view. I was talking to her about a man she had just interviewed for a book on prayer. One person in particular bothered her. "When this guy goes jogging in the morning," she told me with exasperation, "he prays for the people living in the houses he passes." Mary thought this guy had prayer all wrong. It was "prayer as magic," she said with distaste. Prayer was the encounter of soul with God, she believed, not coming to him with a list of things needing manipulating or fixing, things God already sees and knows. Only grade-school piety "tells God what to do."

It is true enough that sometimes we are tempted to use prayer as a kind of magic wand. We want growth without cost, results without effort, answers without asking. Sometimes our asking is little more than panicked cries for a quick God fix.

But that does not negate the place of proper asking. God has willingly chosen to act through us and through our asking. How many times have I kept a list of things to ask for, only to come back and read it weeks or months later and be amazed at how many requests seemed *answered*! God wants to enlist us in his plans, inviting us to participate through prayer. Of course he is powerful enough not to have to call on our puny muscle and stuttering prayers, and he already knows what we tell him. But for our sakes and for the sake of others he becomes the Great Delegator. He allows us to participate with him in what is and what is to come.

C. S. Lewis articulated the struggle to grasp this in this way:

> "Praying for specific things," said I, "always seems like advising God how to run the world. Wouldn't it be better to assume that he knows best?" "On the same principle," said he, "I suppose you never ask the man next to you to pass the salt, because God knows best whether you ought to have salt or not. And I suppose you never take an umbrella because God knows best whether you ought to be wet or dry." "That's quite different," I protested. "I don't see why," said he. "The odd thing is that He should let us influence the course of events at all. But since he lets us do it in one way, I don't see why He shouldn't let us do it in another."[1]

God fiercely defends our right to participate with him in the way things turn out. He does not dictate all that happens. He absorbs our eager longings into his purposes and holy creativity. He puts the exercise of his power at least faintly at our disposal.

Perhaps this is no better fleshed out than in an ancient story. Picture a halting, tongue-tied ancient Hebrew leader named Moses. He quakes when he senses God near. His knees knock. He stutters. But look at him: arguing with God. While Moses confers with God on Mount Sinai, receiving the Ten Commandments, the people in the valley melt their gold to fashion an idol. God almost seems unable to believe it. "I have seen these people," he tells Moses as Moses is about to head back down, "and they are a stiff-necked people. Now leave me alone so that my anger may burn against your people. . . ."

"But Moses sought the favor of the Lord his God," we read. Here is what he prays: "O Lord . . . , why should your anger burn against your people, whom you brought out of Egypt with great power and a mighty hand? . . . Turn from your fierce anger; relent and do not bring disaster on your people."

Then a remarkable conclusion: "The Lord relented and he did not bring on his people the disaster he had threatened" (Exodus 32:9–14 passim).

In so many ways God seems to prefer to work through the slow, the steady, the *human*, rather than through fiat and thunderclap. In prayer we take hold of his willingness to listen and move; we exercise our right as children to influence a loving parent.

This seems almost too good. It boggles the imagination of many people I know. They cannot see it. But their hesitation springs from misunderstanding. Either God wills something, they reason, in which case he will bring it about anyway. Or he does not will something, and their asking can't change anything.

But there is another option: that God both intends for some particular thing to happen *and* wants to use us to make it happen. Perhaps on some things that he wants and plans to do he even *waits* for our prayers before he releases his full blessing. Why not? Yes, it confers on us incredible, even exhilarating opportunity. But we are made, after all, in God's image. When I stop to consider the opportunity he gives us, it marshals forth a palpable thirst to ask. Think of it! *We can make a difference.*

And it confers on us responsibility. He takes our offerings—our thoughtful but small check written to help feed the hungry, our quiet smile of encouragement, and, no less, our praying—to transfigure the world and unfold unimaginable purposes. Jesus said not only to ask, seek, and knock, but that if we do, we will find a door open. That points not only to a promise of what can happen, it suggests what may *not* happen if we ignore the invitation. The world does not face an impersonal fate; God is on the move, and he's enlisting us in his kingdom's advance.

This has been a great and freeing insight to me. I grew up in a Christian denomination that tends to downplay the role of the supernatural in God's way of dealing with humankind. I often heard the maxim "Prayer doesn't change things, it changes *us*." And who can argue with the conviction that prayer can and should deepen us? But it was also often said as though that is *all* prayer accomplished. It was almost the idea, as one popular spirituality book suggests, that prayer is "just talking to" yourself and "reprogramming" your internal computer.[2]

When I enrolled in a hospital-chaplaincy apprenticeship program in seminary, the subject of praying for patients came up in our training group. "I pray out loud with a patient when he or she asks for it," my chaplaincy supervisor told us. "The patient often finds it emotionally therapeutic." For him that was about it: It made patients feel better, but it did nothing to influence God or shape the outcome of events.

But prayer does much more than reassure us when we are needy. God stands in relation to the world as an artist whose work of art shows in every stroke or chip the contribution of an apprentice.[3]

Prayer changes things, not because it is a magical formula but because behind it is nothing less than the exercise of the Creator's power. Prayer moves the hand that holds the universe. God places himself at our disposal not because he is cowed by us or our demands but because he chooses to do so. There is more to our asking than we can ever imagine, because there is more to God than we can ever fathom.

Still a mystery remains. Why does God choose to give us through our praying a role in what happens? Ultimately the best answer must turn not to the vocabulary of philosophy but to the language of relationship.

I ask things of my wife—to hold me when I'm needy, to hear me confess my hidden insecurities—that I would never ask of a stranger or my next-door neighbor. And if I never turned to her for what only she can give, she would know something was gravely wrong. Asking, then, often points to the deepest intimacy. Is it so very different with God? Why do we so fear that we will insult God by our requests? Asking demonstrates that we need him, that we believe God can help us. Such prayers are born of trust. They point to our hope that our lives are held in the arms of a personal presence, not caught in the random processes of impersonal events. God chooses to use our praying because asking always puts us in touch with Another.

On the other side of our asking is God's answering.

When talking about asking prayer, Jesus directed our eyes to a caring parent: "Which of you, if his son asks for bread, will give him a stone? Or if he asks for a fish, will give him a snake? If you, then, though you are evil, know how to give good gifts to your children, how much more will your Father in heaven give good gifts to those who ask him!" (Matthew 7:9–10). I respond when my children ask me for help on a school project, bring me a wish list for a birthday, or reach out for a bedtime hug. I may not always deem their requests possible or advisable. I won't always give them what they request. But I will allow, expect, and even welcome their asking.

Ask my friend Charlene Baumbich, a midwestern free-lance writer, if she has had any recent memorable experiences of asking prayer, and she will tell you of a summer day that had dawned hot, humid, and oppressive. It was a great day to stay in air-conditioned comfort, especially for someone with her history of passing out on blistering days. But she had volunteered through the Kiwanis Club to chaperone some physically challenged children on a trip to the local zoo. "Here I was supposed to be pushing a wheelchair and they were going to need one for me," she told me. As she was getting ready, she called to ask a couple of friends to pray for her stamina. And she prayed for herself. She *asked*.

When she arrived at the group's meeting place, she discovered that one child's mom had decided at the last minute to accompany her child on the outing. Suddenly there was no need for Charlene. "I have no doubt," she told me, "that God moved that other mother to go along. He answered my prayer—better than I would have dared to ask for. And perhaps he was answering that mother's prayer—for a chance to get out of the house, for time to bond with her child. I asked, and he answered."

Asking only becomes magic, I believe, when we try to wield prayer apart from an intimate relationship with God. It is no talisman, no Aladdin's bottle to rub, no formula hatched in the dark womb of magical arts. When we seek the gifts apart from the hand of the giver, when we ask only to gain advantage, when we ignore the face of the one to whom we turn, then something has gone awry. Then we ask wrongly. But that is not the sin of asking; it is more fundamentally the sin of trying to use God, apart from loving him.

There is another way in which asking is crucial. And it is best illustrated by something that happened to me the other day.

That morning I awoke filled with stress, worried about deadlines at the office, centered on myself. The night before, my wife commented on how distant and self-absorbed I had seemed throughout the evening. Even my praying that morning focused on what I needed to get done, what I was feeling, the fears I was nursing. But then, as I kept praying, I began remembering the many people I wanted to pray for. I prayed for my wife. I lifted up the names of my children. I prayed for my mother's need to know that God was near. I remembered a relative who was struggling with doubt and disbelief. I even prayed for the company I work for. Before I knew it, I found my prayers taking me out of myself. I became aware of a wider world around me. Asking pulled me out of my self-absorption.

Asking prayer ideally has two thrusts: First, *petition*, where we pray for ourselves, where we run the gamut from asking for a new house to asking God to make us more faithful. Because God cares about us and our needs, he does not mind entertaining our intensely personal petitions. Second is *intercession*, where we pray for others. Because God cares about those we care about, it is only natural for us to intercede for them. Intercession comes from two Latin words, *inter*, which means "between," and *cedere*, which means "to go." To intercede is to go between two people in the hope of reconciling differences or to plead with someone on behalf of the other. In the context of prayer it means we make sure we bring others into our times of conversation with God. Both kinds of asking are eminently appropriate.

As to *how* we ask, the form can be quite simple. Many people appear in my prayers as "that person lying on the roadside beside a wrecked car" or "the scared woman I saw on the news tonight." I need not wax eloquent or "say it all." One friend of mine depends on God to help him form his intercessions. He sits quietly, meditatively, until God brings gently to his mind those persons or situations that need prayer. Ellis Peters, in her medieval whodunit *A Morbid Taste for Bones*, paints this scene: "He prayed as he breathed, forming no words and making no specific requests, only holding in his heart, like broken birds in cupped hands, all those people who were in stress or grief."[4] I once read of a woman confined to a bed who kept a "family album" of some two hundred photographs of friends, missionaries, and others she wanted to pray for. She worked her way through the entire album each week, praying over the pictures. And I have a friend who jogs her memory to pray for people undergoing surgery or some trial by writing down the date and time of the event in her Day-Timer calendar. That way she is sure to pray for the person in his or her actual hour or moment of need.

I find I can pray for people whenever I think of them, wherever I am. Simple prayers of "help so-and-so," or "be with my neighbor right now," are perfectly acceptable and welcomed by God.

I also try to do more than occasional or random prayers. Because of the truth of the Chinese proverb that the finest mind is less reliable than the simplest ink, I do best if I do not always leave my petitions and intercessions to memory. I keep a list of prayer concerns, and as near as I can come to it, I sit down with it daily. At any given time I have a couple of dozen names and concerns to review. Every so often I cross out an answered prayer or an issue that has passed, starting over with a new list every few months (though some names—those of the people I'm closest to—stay on the list season after season). I pray for my work, for more patience, for greater love for God, for the writing of this book. But it is mostly names, the people who crowd into my life, that I feel called to remember in prayer.

And I try to do more than rush through a recital of mere names. I like to pause and articulate not only the obvious need, but to go deeper, to uncover new layers of what the person I know or care about must be experiencing. I especially try to pray graciously for those who have hurt or angered me. Pat Bailey, an Illinois friend of mine, likes to say, "Take the things you see in people that annoy you and turn them into prayer. God shows you sin and brokenness in people not so that you can criticize and judge them, but so that you can pray for them."

I also try to pray with a global perspective. Starving

masses, wars in far-flung countries, even moral decline in this country, all find a place in my prayer. The New Testament urges "that requests, prayers, intercession, and thanksgiving be made for everyone—for kings and all those in authority, that we may live peaceful and quiet lives . . ." (2 Timothy 2:1–2). There is something very satisfying about prayer that lifts me out of my daily round. Can I measure the impact of my praying against the juggernaut of world violence? The pernicious power of infectious disease? The pervasiveness of poverty? No. But who knows how God uses it? Perhaps, as writer Frank Laubach once suggested, the prayers of people are like the stones filling a swamp that, one by one, a hundred by hundred, seem to do little good, until at last a stone appears on the surface and the swamp disappears.

How does such praying "work"? Not as a function of some impersonal force "activated" by our asking. And just as clearly, prayer's influence does not ignore human choice. Perhaps our prayers for people mostly lower the threshold of their own openness to God or to some new set of circumstances. They may serve to unlock a gate, but they do not coerce someone to walk through it. God's response to our prayers does not violate a person's ability to choose. Yet, I believe, in our prayers lies great power, the power of the God who invites us to pray in the first place because he wants to use our asking.

Asking makes spiritual sense in one more way. It saturates our lives with a sense of possibility. "Humankind stands at a crossroads," someone once said. "One way leads to despair and hopelessness. The other to total destruction. Pray that we have the wisdom to choose correctly." Prayer reminds us that we need never despair. The one to whom we appeal is a God of justice and power and love. In prayer we participate as hopeful subversives against the powers of darkness and evil.

When your child has run away, your job has been stolen out from under you, your relationship with God has gone dry and barren, when a little boy is hounded and hurt because of the color of his skin, praying reminds us that all is not hopeless. It reminds us that even when we feel powerless, we can turn to someone who is able to do beyond our ability to think and even imagine.

One Saturday morning my wife and I lingered over breakfast, reading the morning newspaper. As Jill flipped through the section with local news, an ad caught her eye. A church was announcing its pastor's message for the following morning's worship service. The title was intriguing: "Don't Be Afraid to Ask."

I didn't hear that sermon, but what struck me with an instant, clean force was the title's rightness as an invitation to prayer. Don't be afraid, our greatest mentors in the faith tell us, don't ever hesitate to ask. Come as you are, with all your clamoring requests. But don't do so lightly: you will not likely stay the same. Nor will the world around you.

Prayers

Lord, I am ready for you to use my praying. Guide my thoughts that I will know how to pray. Guide my lips that I will ask for those things that give you glory. And remind me that you can use my requests to change the world. Amen.

We bring before you, O Lord, the troubles and perils of people and nations, the sighing of prisoners and captives, the sorrows of the bereaved, the necessities of strangers, the helplessness of the weak, the despondency of the weary, the failing powers of the aged. O Lord, draw near to each; for the sake of Jesus Christ our Lord.

—ANSELM (ELEVENTH CENTURY)[5]

Part Three

How We Keep Going

8

Getting Real with God: Emotions in Prayer

Do not let it be imagined that one must remain silent about one's feelings of rebellion in order to enter into dialogue with God. Quite the opposite is the truth: it is precisely when one expresses them that a dialogue of truth begins.

—PAUL TOURNIER

I have risen against His justice, protested His silence and sometimes his absence, but my anger rises up within faith and not outside it. . . . [I]t is permissable for man to accuse God, provided it be done in the name of faith in God.

—ELIE WIESEL

The Prayer of Complaint. . . . has been largely lost in our modern, sanitized religion, but the Bible abounds with it.

—RICHARD FOSTER

From the beginning of our romance, my wife and I have easily expressed to each other tender feelings and wishes. Sometimes we animatedly discuss the details of our jobs and family; other times we expose corners of our deeper selves. By far our toughest times for communicating are when one of us is angry. Early in our courtship was the hardest of all. When incensed, Jill would sometimes walk away—literally. My strategy looked more mannered but was just as destructive: I would go inside myself, clam up. Jill and I had to learn how to argue. We needed lessons in how to be angry without withdrawing. We had to find ways to channel our fuming or offended feelings.

I believe something similar takes place in prayer. When we get mad at God for something we think God could have helped us avoid, we are tempted to walk away or pull back. We are not sure our churning emotions belong in the presence of God. We become reserved, and often not too motivated to pray.

I believe our emotions—all of them—belong in our prayers. "If we are without human feelings," writes contemplative writer Thomas Merton, "we cannot love God in the way in which we are meant to love him—as [human beings]."[1] Our prayers represent not just what we say but who we are, with all our complex longings and feelings. To be close to someone, even when that someone is God, will inevitably run us through a gamut of emotions. To think prayer should be a monochrome patter is to rob it of its power. To read the Psalms or other devotional outpourings of prayers classical and contemporary is to witness a dazzling emotional tapestry. A wide and sometimes wild range of feelings accompanies a walk with God.

So we can be real with God. And because most of us know that we can exult with adoration, or bow our heads in contrition, or intently, urgently ask, this chapter will look at what troubles us more: our disappointment with God, the anger that sometimes makes us stew or smolder or grow away from him.

The subject is not merely academic for me. Some years ago, when my wife and I had moved to a suburb to start a new church, things weren't happening as we had hoped. I sometimes felt trapped by expectations—mine, those of church members, and those who had commissioned us to go. While I believed God had led us to Houston, he didn't seem all that interested in making things "work." This is how I described one morning in my journal: "I awoke feeling mad at God. I didn't want to pray or read Scripture. I saw my Scripture memory verses by the bedside and an image of my stomach turning flashed through my mind. I thought of praying several times during the day, but recoiled at the idea. The whole process leaves me depressed, but my anger—or desire to keep God at a distance—seems to paralyze me."

Our first reaction may be to shrink from such feelings. They seem very "unprayerful." But we do better to admit and acknowledge—not submerge—them. We can consider later where they should take us. For now we are the wiser if we bring them out into view.

Cathy Kelly, an articulate, committed believer, a mother, and a biologist, managed to do that in the wake of her divorce after ten years of marriage:

> I went through a nightmare of emotions, from sorrow and despair to frustration and rage. My "prayer life" as I was used to it became nonexistent. I found I could *not* pray—not in the way I believed prayer had to be done. Oh, I could "pray" the Psalms—I was living the Psalms! But all other prayers became dry, impossible. What I found myself doing throughout that long summer was questioning—my faith, my God, my purpose for being. I found myself one night absolutely ranting and raging at God, asking him . . . no, *telling* him what I thought of the whole situation. I demanded that he show himself to me.
>
> I was horrified with myself the next day, wondering if I had committed a sin by being so "truthful." But a good friend pointed out to me that my ranting was probably the closest I had come in a long time to true prayer.

Much in Christian tradition—the Psalms, with their frequent outbursts of anger against enemies; the prophets, with their plaintive, impatient questioning of God—recognizes, as we often fail to do, the pervasiveness of anger. Unlike some in the ancient world, who made a lack of passion a key virtue, our mentors in the faith respected emotions. They were not interested in sanitizing life. They knew emotions needed expression, even—perhaps especially—anger. Sometimes we need to vent.

"I never found a blissful peace to disappear into," Cathy remembers of her angry praying. "My life continued to be a challenging disarray of routine, of insecurity, of emotion. But I found that I was sustained in many ways by God's grace— not in any concrete way that can be categorized, but things 'happened,' good things that might have only been coincidences except I believe there are no coincidences with God." Had she "broken through" that night she "ranted"? Had her finally acknowledging what she felt let her once again approach God instead of avoid him?

But, we worry, *Wouldn't we be offending a righteous, holy God?* Some, recalling Jesus' words about the "blasphemy against the Holy Spirit" (Matthew 12:32), fear that yelling at God is the "unforgivable sin" to which Jesus referred.

That fear is easily set to rest. The "blasphemy" against the Holy Spirit that troubles some people's conscience is not railing at God. It refers rather to those in Jesus' own day who rejected the Spirit's work in him even though they should have known better. It has to do with icy *unbelief*, not hot anger. Not with what we say so much as our basic disposition toward God. To blaspheme is to utterly reject, not to howl in pain.

Indeed, anger is often the first sign that we care. And just as a couple's constructive anger need not detonate their marriage, so also is our impatience with God hardly enough to send him running. He does not ask us to walk on eggshells around him. He is a jealous God, as the Bible says, but not oversensitive. So, as my friend Charlene Baumbich tells me, "Box, fight, scream, holler, cry, give thanks, and praise. Tell God everything that's on your mind, because he knows anyway."

God would rather have us come angry than not come at all. For then at least we are angry in his presence rather than pushing him away in our isolation. Better mad than removed. Emotion, even strong negative emotion, keeps us in contact with God.

And sometimes letting something boil over, rather than letting it steam and simmer, gets us through the time more cleanly. The petulant anger of my Texas journal entry was short-lived; had I never written it down, it would be lost from memory. Yet was it my writing it down and facing my anger that helped me not be troubled by it for long?

Anger with God, I believe, is not the same as abandoning God. Whole sections of the Psalms are crowded with complaint and lament. And yet note: They always find expression as *prayers*. The protest is couched, as Jewish novelist and essayist Elie Wiesel writes,[2] in the name of faith in God:

But I cry out to you for help, O Lord;
>   in the morning my prayer comes before you.
Why, O Lord, do you reject me
>   and hide your face from me? (Psalm 88:13–14)

Such prayers express the psalmist's hurt and pathos. As does this psalm:

My God, my God, why have you forsaken me?
>   Why are you so far from saving me,
>   so far from the words of my groaning?
O my God, I cry out by day, but you do not answer,
>   by night, and am not silent. (Psalm 22:1–2)

The indignant words are *addressed to God*. The moaning is sandwiched in between the saying of God's name. The context is the God to whom we turn in our hurt: "O God, *whom I praise*, do not remain silent" (Psalm 109:1).

These psalms, and other prayers like them, writes Richard Foster, "teach us to pray our inner conflict and contradictions. They allow us to shout out our forsakenness in the dark caverns of abandonment and then hear the echo return to us over and over until we . . . recant of them, only to shout them out again. They give us permission to shake our fist at God one moment and break into [praise] again the next."[3]

And they teach us that anger usually gives way to praise. It is hard to be sullen for long when addressing a good God.

———

A friend went through significant disappointment with her childbearing. For years she was infertile. Finally she conceived and delivered two healthy children, but then miscarried twice within six months. To Karen's grief, the doctor finally told her she should not have any more children. "I felt God was saying, 'I want good things for you,' at the same time that he was letting awful things happen to me."

Finally, she told me,

I lost hope. I started asking, "Why do I believe in God? *Is* there a God?" A Christian friend came to visit me in the hospital to talk and pray with me. While he talked, I thought, *I don't believe a word you are saying.* I felt no one understood the pain I was in. Then I began to think about my life before I knew God. And I realized that to go back to my "pagan" life would lead to even greater despair.

Finally, in desperation I cried out to God, "I'm in pain. I'm angry at you. But out of faith I will follow you."

At that point I sensed a presence in the room unlike any I had ever sensed. Then I glimpsed a mental picture of the Lord in the room with me. In the vision I was on the floor in a puddle of pain. But the Lord put his arms around me in a strong embrace. He lifted me to my feet. He began to dance with me.

Karen allowed her anger to turn her to God. Once she got near him, the picture changed. She came through to the other side.

That is how it happens in the Psalms. The cries and protests come out of faith, so they lead back to faith. One moment the pray-er is crying out in forsakenness: "You do not answer." The next he is affirming: "Yet . . ."

Yet you are enthroned as the Holy One;
    you are the praise of Israel.
In you our fathers put their trust;
    they trusted and you delivered them.
They cried out to you and were saved;
    in you they trusted and were not disappointed.
    (Psalm 22:4–5)

I like the story of how a journalist made a discovery similar to the psalmist's. While on a photojournalism assignment in Virginia early on a June morning in 1984, Frank Bianco learned that Michael, one of his two sons, had been killed in a car collision. Already wavering in his religious faith, Frank used the tragedy to blame God bitterly.

Almost immediately Bianco also experienced a cruel twist of the grieving process: He had a bizarre amnesia when it came to Michael. All memories of his son vanished. But weeks later, when a writing assignment took him to a monastery, something else happened:

When I entered [the monastery's church], about fifty white- and black-robed monks were already in their choir stalls directly below. Five minutes later they were standing, facing forward, when a knock signaled them to begin.

I do not recall particular words or phrases from the liturgy that followed. I know I was struck by the monks' genuine reverence. They were not mouthing rituals. They were singing carefully, slowly, as one disciplined voice. They were talking to someone. I did not doubt that any more than I would doubt the presence of a catcher if I were watching a pitcher winding up.

I glanced around the church, looking for that catcher. But the tabernacle was not glowing. Nor was the crucifix over the altar moving. And the light streaming through the stained-glass windows did not alter a bit. No, everything was perfectly normal. With one exception. For the first time since he had died, memories of Michael began to flood my mind.

Whenever Bianco returned to a church setting, the memories flooded back. Once outside the building, the memories vanished again.

And still Bianco raged at God. One day, after pouring out his pain and grief and anger while he stood in a worship service, Bianco realized, "The God I had reviled and rejected had been waiting to mourn with me, burned with sorrow he would share with me. I felt so ashamed. I had been so wrong, for so long. Yet God had never given up on me. . . . I heard the words, 'I know, I know. As you did, as you still do, I love him too. I know.' "

That was the turning point in his anger. He discovered that God hurt with him. "I stayed [in the church]," Bianco concluded, "weeping, as the pain poured out. But not alone. Not unconsoled. This time I wept in the arms of my God, whom I finally allowed to hold me in that monastery church."[4]

Prayer is an expression of who we *are*. And how we pray is part of a complex of emotions, outlooks, experiences, and psychological patterns. Even when we think we are suppressing what is going on underneath, who we are and what we are feeling and thinking affects what happens. If we stay with our anger instead of running from it, it will lead us into an intimacy with God deeper than we have ever known.

Not long after Jill and I became engaged, we had a huge fight. I vividly remember her and me sitting on a park bench in the Princeton, New Jersey, sunshine. She was fingering her diamond engagement ring, and I expected her to hand it back to me any minute. I don't recall the specifics of our anger, just that it had to do with the normal stresses of joining two very separate lives, and that the emotions were intense. But something kept us at it. Through our tears and letting down our guard and sharing our honest frustrations, our relationship avoided meltdown. We decided we liked each other again. In our talking it through, we saw that what drove us apart should not quench our love. We got up from the bench and started walking together. We have kept going ever since.

I'm glad, angry words and all, that we came out on the other side. And our relationship, still with occasional tiffs, continues to weather the challenges—as a strong marriage should. As prayer can.

Prayers

Lord, you know the swirl of emotions within me.
>   *Help me not let my disappointment drive me away from*
>   *you.*
>   *Help me to be honest, and yet not get stuck in my*
>   *frustration.*
Amen.

Why, O Lord, do you stand far off?
>   *Why do you hide yourself in times of trouble? . . .*
Arise, Lord! Lift up your hand, O God.
>   *Do not forget the helpless. . . .*
You hear, O Lord, the desire of the afflicted;
>   *you encourage them, and you listen to their cry.*

—PSALM 10:1, 12, 17

9

Listening for God in Our Lives

The moment you wake up each morning, . . . [a]ll your wishes and hopes for the day rush at you like wild animals. And the first job each morning consists in shoving them all back; in listening to that other voice, taking that other point of view, letting that other, larger, stronger, quieter life come flowing in.

—C. S. LEWIS

A man prayed, and at first he thought the prayer was talking. But he became more and more quiet until in the end he realized that prayer is listening.

—SØREN KIERKEGAARD

*An inner, secret turning to God can be made fairly
steady, after weeks and months and years of practice and
lapses and failures and returns.*

—*THOMAS KELLY*

Not long ago I was driving to work, praying about the day
ahead. I included in my mental list the phone calls I needed
to return, a child sick at home, and my concerns about a
manuscript I needed to edit. I suddenly realized how much
my praying was filled with items on my life's agenda. I realized how little time I spend simply *listening* to God. I felt
moved to stop talking. For the rest of my trip I made
myself—my heart and my ears—available to God. What
a significant shift! I received no dazzling insight, but I felt
as though suddenly I was tuned in to God, not just bending
his ear.

I know people, though, who are wary of listening prayer.
Who believe God would never deign to speak, except perhaps to near-saints. I know others who greet the very idea
with skepticism, who think hearing from God is akin to contact with extraterrestrials. And who doesn't know of terrible
things done in the name of "God told me to"? During the
"God is dead" movement of the sixties and seventies, evan-
gelist Billy Graham once said he was sure God existed
because he had talked to him that morning. "Ah, but that is
not the issue," one theologian countered. "The question is,
Did God talk back?"

But if God is not a mute deity, why wouldn't he speak? If
he is wondrously personal, why should our praying be a

monologue? And "why is it," asks comedienne Lily Tomlin, "that when we speak to God we are said to be praying, but when God speaks to us we are said to be schizophrenic?"[1] Yes, people get the message garbled. But that does not mean he does not communicate. Through written revelation, angels, miracles, a still, small voice, and the murmurs of conscience, God does not keep silent. Which means prayer must entail more than our talking.

A friend of mine likes to say that he does his best praying when he *stops* praying—when he shuts his mouth long enough to hear something more than his own urgent rambling.

So how do we do it?

We Listen Prayerfully to Our Lives

If God is present in the world, he is surely present in what happens to us. He unfolds his will for us in life's little moments, its turns and detours, its bright moments and dark. Daily events (and nonevents) are a kind of alphabet through which God communicates. We get a job offer out of the blue that changes our career direction. Somebody tells us something we don't want to hear, but need to. A parent we thought had written us off calls to struggle out the words "I am proud of you." We piece together the "letters" and suddenly see something we might have missed.

So we pray not only for what we want to see happen but about what actually does happen. We attend to our lives as they are. As they already have been. We "read life backward" for clues about where we should go. We try to see what God is saying. We recognize that we can learn much simply by listening to what transpires around and within us.

I find keeping a journal one of the best ways to do that. Journaling is not so much recording the day's or week's minutiae so much as setting down what happens to me in light of my relationship with God. It is a prayerful discipline for me. It allows me to reflect on my ordinary experiences. I don't write every day, but I do try to write a page or two every so often. Then every few months I flip back to earlier entries, and I am reminded of a promise God gave me, or a new direction I sensed opening up, or a friend's encouraging word. When I find themes being repeated over the years, I recognize patterns that give me direction, remind me where I'm going.

Journaling, of course, is not the only way to listen to our lives. Simply by being more reflective, more alert, we can read life's clues.

We Learn to Listen Through Pain

Sometimes we see suffering as an interruption or distraction. It even drives us to question God's existence. But there is another view.

Here is Madeleine L'Engle, renowned author, living through the slow, agonizing death of her husband. She finds four lines of poetry from William Butler Yeats and copies them down:

But Love has pitched his mansion in
The place of excrement;
For nothing can be sole or whole
That has not been rent.

"This summer," she reflected in her journal, "is not the first time I have walked through the place of excrement and found love's mansion there. Indeed, we are more likely to find it in the place of excrement than in the sterile places. God comes where there is pain and brokenness."[2]

When we are rent and hurting, we may for the first time open our ears and our hearts. Pain wakes us up. "God whispers to us in our pleasures, speaks in our consciences, but shouts in our pain: it is his megaphone to rouse a deaf world," said C. S. Lewis.[3] I wish it weren't so, but it is often disappointment or panic that drives me to my knees. Suffering opens us to hear something that in our stiffness and pride and self-sufficiency we would otherwise never bother with.

I once heard of a minister who said he had mixed feelings about praying for the physical healing of his church members' ailments, because the illnesses were so good for their souls. Many people finally slow down enough to listen only when flat on their back in bed. Or only when the pain inside makes them ask some deeper questions. Our hurts often lead us to God. They bring us to moments of healthy questioning.

M.S., a forty-four-year-old Louisianan, tells this story:

My husband and I were going through a terrible crisis. I was very fearful of our future and praying off and on all day and night. . . . One morning, in a half-asleep, half-awake state, I kept hearing three musical notes in my head [that made me] . . . very calm and peaceful. I finally awakened fully and while dressing realized that the tune in my head was a song I had sung in choir when I was in high school twenty years earlier. The words that accompany those three notes are "Trust in God." Was it a dream or a message? I took it as a message, and though the crisis we were in did not change for another seven months, I was never as fearful or worried again. When the crisis ended, the outcome was much better than I ever dreamed possible.[4]

We Learn to Listen by Asking for Guidance

One of the most significant and profound ways to begin our prayer times is to tell God we are listening. That we are ready for him to speak. I have always been moved by the Bible's young Samuel. His guardian, the temple priest Eli, coached the boy on listening: "If [God] calls you, say, 'Speak, Lord, for your servant is listening' " (1 Samuel 3:9).

When my life lacks a clear focus, or I need guidance, or I simply want to be more open to God, I find it helpful to remember this story. Somehow this recollection prepares my heart when God finally does speak. God may not tell me everything I wish to know, but he is able to tell more than if I was not alert and attuned.

And when I listen in this way, I will often find an answer on an impending decision growing more certain. A sense of "rightness" will emerge. I don't get it right every time of course, but something inside me says, *Yes, this is God's best.* Or I will suddenly be prompted to pray for someone, only to find out later that the individual was at that moment experiencing crisis and desperately needed prayer support. If I am open, God can influence me, hiddenly or visibly.

I also believe God may influence and speak without our knowing it. I notice a gentle restraint in much of God's communicating with us. God seems to favor the quiet and unobtrusive. We often think celestial fireworks are a surer sign—that if we have seen a "big" miracle, we must have really heard. But God is communicating all the time. Only if we are especially deaf will he have to resort to angels or heavenly skywriting. Angel messages, blinding lights, and roadside burning bushes are not his preferred modes. God's speaking may be no more dramatic than my being reminded that I am being held and watched through every circumstance.

Occasionally, God seems to use the unusual to guide us. I have a friend I'll call Betty Rogers. She has been single for years, ever since her marriage ended in painful divorce. The failure of her marriage caused great emotional pain, intensified by her religious convictions that found divorce abhorrent. Betty did not want to face the rest of her life consigned to singleness, yet she also did not want to marry if it was contrary to God's best intentions. She now has told me she has her answer: "I recently came to a place in my life where I said, 'Okay, God, I'm ready to hear from you what your will is on all this.' I did not know what to expect, and if God had said no, I was not going to ask again. I would have remained single for the rest of my life."

But the night of her prayer for guidance she had a dream. In the first part she simply felt a sensation of safety and protection, all the more significant because of abuse in her former marriage. But then the dream took an oddly funny turn. She could see actor John Goodman, "in all of his portliness," standing with a silly grin on his face and his arms outstretched. In her dream Betty hesitantly came to him and received an embrace.

Betty, no fan of Goodman, would have thought nothing more of the dream, except that she felt an inner prompting to go to a dictionary and look up the word *goodman*. To her amazement she found that it was an archaic word for *husband*. She took that odd discovery as God's leading. She heard no timetable or name of whom she might marry, but she felt she had her answer: God will someday provide for her a "goodman."

Of course we may hear no celestial sound bite. God may not say anything in particular. Dan Rather once interviewed Mother Teresa of Calcutta. "What do you say to God when you pray?" he asked. Mother Teresa looked at him with her dark, soulful eyes and said quietly, "I listen." Slightly flus-

tered, Rather tried again. "Well, then, what does God say?"
Mother Teresa smiled. "He listens."[5] Profound communication can often take place in the subtlest of ways, through a
still, small voice.

We Listen by Paying Attention to Revealed Truth

Much of listening is simply absorbing the truth and presence
of God. Especially at the beginning, when we are learning
how to discern God's voice, we need not place heavy expectations upon ourselves. We needn't worry too much about
abundant revelations.

In fact I believe God speaks most clearly through the life,
death, and resurrection of Jesus—the Word made flesh, as
the Bible calls him. God speaks through the recorded revelations of the prophets and sages and apostles of Scripture. He
speaks through the wisdom of history's great spiritual
teachers. Much of my prayer for guidance leads me there.
Much of listening is taking to heart what I already know or
what God has already given.

For in spite of our culture's penchant for rugged individualism and frontier independence, there is much we cannot cal-
culate and find on our own. We cannot philosophize our way
to truth. When we try, we end up confused and be-
fuddled, or just plain wrong. We need to listen to what God
tells us through God's written Word, the Bible, and the Living
Word, Jesus, in whom, says Paul, "all the fullness of the Deity

lives in bodily form" (Colossians 2:9). We are not left to our own devices when it comes to understanding what is true.

I was intrigued to find that behind our word *absurd* lies the Latin root *surdus*, which means "deaf." In our deafness, in our occasional reluctance to open to truth outside ourselves, our lives become absurd. By way of contrast, our word *obedient* comes from a Latin word for "listening." We move from absurdity to obedience, from floundering confusion to conformity to God's will, through listening.

This is where Scripture can guide. God "chose to give us birth through the word of truth" (James 1:18). We can't just stand under the stars and let our ruminations guide us to God. We read. We listen. We are taught. We let our words be formed by the words others used before us. And we spend time getting to know the one whom we address. That may happen no more thoroughly than through absorbing what he has already told us about himself through the Bible. Writes Peter in the New Testament,

> "All men are like grass,
>   and all their glory is like the flowers of the field;
> the grass withers and the flowers fall,
>   but the word of the Lord stands forever."
> And this is the word that was preached to you.
>   (1 Peter 1:22–25)

I try to ensure, then, that Scripture is part of my praying. But I try to read meditatively, not trying to plow through a long section as much as let what is written find root in me. If

I do not understand all I read, I go on, but note a question to ask someone more knowledgeable sometime. I try to allow the truth of the Bible to become my truth.

This need not be an elaborate affair. I try to read a chapter and a psalm each morning. The state of my schedule and my discipline being what it is, I don't always manage it. And when I don't, I try at least to call up a memorized verse or passage. The goal is to allow God's truth to keep us from getting off track. One does not need a graduate degree to understand Scripture's simple words. At the same time, classes from wise and knowledgeable teachers can go a long way in helping us deepen our understanding.

Then I often *pray* what I've read. I ask God to reveal himself indeed as my shepherd. Or to make real a lesson in trusting God I may have read about in a story like Abraham's. This "talking back" to God includes questions where fuller understanding is needed—"Lord, what are you saying to me today?"—as well as prayers of thanksgiving and praise, and petitions for wisdom and guidance through what I have read.

Then I open myself to what God might want to say. God comes at his own initiative, not our conjuring, but we should not close our minds. So we face the potentially unnerving prospect that God may indeed want to tell us something. Or we listen with an uncontainable delight when God reminds us that he cares enough not to leave us alone in our decisions and questions.

In listening to God I try to remember that such guidance is sought only as part of a certain kind of life: one of loving, ongoing relationship. It is not fortune-telling we are about, and God's word is not something we call up only when we grow anxious. We do not make our goal extracting specific data on what to expect so much as gaining the Lord's mind. We seek an increase of wisdom in the Spirit.

And then we try to let what we learn stay with us. In the same way that the early-morning words of my wife will sometimes linger in my mind for much of the day, so the word of Scripture and of the Lord can carry me along. It can feed my soul with truth as I walk into the scenes of my life.

Sometimes Scripture will speak to us in a remarkably powerful way. My friend Kevin Miller once told me of the time his father died. His mother called to tell him that his dad had been admitted to the coronary intensive care unit with a massive heart attack. "I went back to my bedroom," Kevin recalled. "I was really upset. But when I opened my Bible, I chanced to open the passage in Matthew 4 that spoke of Jesus' first disciples leaving their fathers to follow him. That phrase hit me. I realized that regardless of what happened with my dad, I had to follow Jesus. I heard a word that helped get me through a difficult time."

Prayers

Lord, you have taught us in your word that there is a time
to speak
and a time to keep silence.
As we thank you for the power of speech,
we pray for the grace of silence.

Make us as ready to listen as we are to talk,
    ready to listen to your voice in the quietness of our hearts
    and ready to listen to other people who need a
        sympathetic ear.
Show us when to open our mouths and when to hold our
        peace
    that we may glorify you both in speech and in silence
    through Jesus Christ our Lord.

—FRANK COLQUHOUN[6]

Lord, help me not to talk over you. Deliver me from chatter. Help me to hear you when you speak in Scripture, help me to see you in Jesus Christ, and enable me to follow all that your Holy Spirit leads me to. Amen.

10

Making Sense of
Unanswered
Prayer

I have lived to thank God that all my prayers have not been answered.

—JEAN INGELOW

Beware, in your prayer, above everything, of limiting God, not only by unbelief, but by fancying that you know what he can do.

—ANDREW MURRAY

Early in the 1980s a friend gave me a biography of nineteenth-century British orphanage founder George Müller. Threadbare, scrawny orphans often begged on the streets of Müller's England. Sometimes they were packed off to workhouse dungeons. Müller decided he had to help. He left his mark on history by pioneering a work that would eventually house and feed thousands of desperate children.

What especially struck me was the way Müller chose to finance his work: prayer. He vowed that he would never talk about a need for food or buildings or money. He would "advertise" the necessities to "no man"—only to God. In spite of some close scrapes, Müller's insistence on turning to God alone in prayer seemed always somehow to "work": In one of many such accounts he gathered the children around a breakfast table set with plates and cups, but no food. After thanking God for the food "you are going to give us to eat," someone knocked on the door. There stood a local baker saying, "I couldn't sleep last night. Somehow I felt you didn't have bread for breakfast, and the Lord wanted you to have some. So I got up at two o'clock and baked some fresh bread." Almost immediately there came a second knock. This time it was a milkman, who announced that his milk cart had broken down outside the orphanage. He wanted the children to have his milk so that he could empty his wagon and repair it.[1] In instance after instance, when funds fell low, without fail an envelope of money would arrive, often just in the nick of time.

At the time Müller's biography arrived, my wife and I were facing some daunting circumstances of our own. We lived on a stringent budget and never seemed to have money enough for each month's bills. As we read about Müller, we remembered a hopeless bill we owed for income taxes. We thought that the due date would present the perfect occasion to put Müller's prayer principle to the test. It could be an eleventh-hour breakthrough, some unforeseen gift or windfall, but if we only asked, we reasoned, an answer would come.

I will never forget the mingled hope and trepidation with which we greeted April 15th. Nor will I forget what actually happened. More precisely, what *didn't* happen.

No check made its way miraculously to our mailbox. No anonymous benefactor called. Our debt would plague us for months. As the day wore on and our prospects for meeting our obligation loomed bleaker, my wife and I wondered if we had misunderstood. Was God not willing to do this sort of thing? Or was it just us?

Practically anyone can tell of similar experiences. Nothing troubles us more than the hurt or anger or confusion left in the wake of a request that God, for all appearances, ignores. Not only will the door not open, it seems closed in our faces. And our requests are so sincere; why the apparent cosmic indifference? The problem of unanswered prayers is one of the most thorny facing those who pray.

On one level, of course, we can all see why sometimes our petitions must go unmet. "If God answered the prayers of dogs," an Arabian proverb has it, "it would rain bones." When two high school basketball teams face off in a state championship game, teammates on both sides pray with all that is in them, making deals with God. We know that such prayers must always end in disappointment for someone. We have no trouble intellectually seeing how granting one side's requests involves refusing that of the other.

But the intellect does not always answer for our feelings. In many experiences of asking, it's hard not to feel snubbed. And the nature of prayer itself doesn't help. Talk to a flesh-and-blood friend, and you can grasp a hand or peer into a pair of eyes. But prayer means addressing a presence we do not tangibly see or touch, a person we rarely—or never—audibly hear. "I feel like Helen Keller in a barrel," someone once confessed to a friend of mine. "Sometimes I feel like my prayers go nowhere." We cry out in agony or desperation, but the silence seems pointed and poignant.

I believe this struggle is both easily resolved and ultimately mysterious. On one level, explaining unanswered prayer means plumbing the depths of the problem of evil and pain; there is much we may never understand. But on another, some simple points can make sense of most of our problems. I will touch on the latter before attacking the former.

Our wrestling with unanswered prayers has to do, first of all, with a lack of clarity about what we can expect. "The real problem," says C. S. Lewis, "is . . . not why refusal is so frequent, but why the opposite result is so lavishly promised."[2] Why is the Bible so unrestrained in its promise of answers? Ask, seek, knock, Jesus said, and you will be answered. "You may ask me for anything in my name," Jesus promised his followers, "and I will do it." So what does seemingly unanswered prayer mean?

We May Fail to Distinguish Between God's Long View and Our Own Sense of Timing

In our day of instant everything, we may be what Sue Monk Kidd calls "quickaholics." Our culture conditions us to think that faster is always better, whether we are getting fitted for eyeglasses or grabbing a hamburger. Even in our spiritual hunger we want microwave convenience. We prefer our answers in celestial sound bites. In some religious quarters, it seems, the more abrupt a prayed-for change in someone, the more certain you can be that you are witnessing the action of God. Suddenness functions as a seal of spiritual authenticity. But while conversion or healing or immersion in the reality of God certainly may happen by fiat, it is often the exception. We must often trust the slow work of God. We must sometimes not give up so easily.

I have planted seeds in a garden many times: pumpkins, beans, zinnias. Almost always they germinate and push up seedlings. When I have to wait and wait, though, I resist the temptation to dig them up every couple of days to see how they are doing. To do so could stunt or kill the tender shoots. In spiritual matters also I have had to learn the value of deliberateness and calm steadiness. I must prepare to wait. I need to expect change in increments. Sometimes God's best answer is "not now" or "wait."

While Jill and I did not get the money we needed for our tax bill when we wanted it, we did manage to pay it off over the following several months. On paper, finding the extra money to pay the IRS looked impossible. But God was faithful. We just had to wait. And to learn some lessons about the long view.

For some things an instant answer is unrealistic. When we pray that we will become more spiritually mature, we should not expect immediate results. We will need to think in terms of months, not moments; decades, not days. A woman shopping at a department store saw a chess set. She approached a clerk and said, "This looks interesting. How do you play it?" Well, some answers are not reducible to a two-minute explanation. God works miracles of immediate transformation in people, but matters such as development of character certainly will not happen in a thunderclap. Pray for patience, and God's answer will likely be to place you in proximity to irritating people around whom you will slowly have to fashion new ways of relating, encounter by encounter. Pray for more faith, and you may find yourself in the kind of situation my wife and I faced with our finances.

So I may have to keep on praying—again and again. Englishman William Carey, a pioneer missionary in the early nineteenth century, once said that if, after his death, anyone found his life worth writing about, there was one criterion by which to judge its correctness: "If he gives me credit for being a plodder he will describe me justly. Anything beyond this will be too much. I can plod. That is my only genius. I can persevere in any definite pursuit. To this I owe everything."[3]

Too often I quit when the answer does not immediately drop from the sky. But wise, spiritual teachers tell us that persistence is a virtue. One of the important things about prayer is to keep at it.

You may pray for years for triumph in yourself over some temptation. You may petition God for justice in some terrible situation. You may ask for a loved one to be saved from addiction. Don't too quickly conclude that a lack of an immediately identifiable answer means that nothing is happening. Keep praying, says Jesus, even when the years turn into decades and you still see no concrete evidence. Some things take time.

We May Not Recognize God's Blessings for What They Are

Sometimes we ask for possessions that would ruin us if we got them. Relationships that would drain us if we entered them. Power that would corrupt us if we got it. The tiny son who sees his mother carving the Thanksgiving turkey may plead for a chance to wield the knife himself. "No," the parent must say. And it may be years before he understands the reason. God treats us too well to give us some of the things we ask for.

We don't always see clearly. We do not always recognize God's answers right off. Sometimes he responds—gloriously—with just what we want. He gives us the desires of our hearts. But that happens most often when our will is in line with his; when it is not, it is graciousness that withholds the desired object.

I like the story of a Chinese farmer who kept an old horse for tilling the fields. One day the horse escaped into the hills. When all the farmer's neighbors sympathized with him over his bad luck, he said, "Bad luck? Good luck? Who knows?"

A week later the horse returned with a herd of wild horses from the hills. This time the neighbors congratulated the farmer on his good luck. "Good luck?" he replied. "Bad luck? Who knows?"

When one of his sons was trying to tame one of the wild horses, he broke his leg. Everyone thought this very bad luck. Not the farmer, whose reaction was simply, "Bad luck? Good luck? Who knows?"

Some weeks later the army marched into the village and conscripted every able-bodied youth they could find. When they saw the farmer's son with his broken leg, they let him off. Now, was that good luck or bad luck? Who knows?

So much that on the surface seems to be misfortune may be a benefit in disguise. And what seems like an unqualified good may cause our devastation. Our perspective is so limited. We are wise when we leave it to God to decide what is good "luck" and bad.

We Mistakenly Value the Object of Our Request More Than the Process

God may be less concerned about answering the petition that forms on our lips than he is with shaping *us*. Prayer does sometimes change us. What drives us to prayer ultimately sets in motion a soul-searching that leaves us different. With time, what we "needed" may not seem so urgent, nor even desirable. As our wills become more conformed to his, what we thought was so prized may pale or even seem wrong. I have prayed for jobs that I later bless God for never getting. But God still brings good because the process of praying itself helps me grow. In the case of my wife and me—praying with all our might for a miraculous influx of cash into our checking account—God had some deeper work to do. He taught us something about walking by faith, not by sight. He also let us learn some practical lessons about managing our finances.

Sometimes, I believe, our problem with seemingly unanswered prayer is a matter of perspective. And in this regard I find it essential not to forget the prayers that already have been answered. Our clinging to our disappointment in a given situation may blind us to the miraculous we have already experienced. We forget the times that prayer "works" gloriously. God *can* move in powerful ways in response to prayer. My friend Jeanie Hunter found that out. She told me this story:

> In 1983 surgery to have a tumor removed from my ear left a facial nerve severely damaged, causing paralysis and weakness on the left side of my face. My hearing was so affected that I had to wear a hearing aid. The nerve controlling taste was cut, so all food tasted like wet cardboard. And my middle ear was injured, leaving in my head a constant ringing. On top of it I was so dizzy I had to spend most of the day in bed or lying on a couch.

On Wednesday, February 11, 1987, someone from my church called and asked if I was going to attend the Wednesday-morning service. I said no: I wasn't feeling well. I had a sofa in my office and I intended to lie down. My friend, however, was not easily put off. She told me that a guest speaker with a healing ministry, Delores Winder, was going to speak. I finally agreed.

As I drove to the church, I could sense a voice saying, "This could be the last time you drive to the church sick." I knew the medical community had done all they could. Could it be possible that God would heal me?

After Delores spoke, I went forward to ask her to pray with me. I explained my condition. She and a handful of prayer counselors prayed with me. My prayer was "Lord, please either heal me or let me die. I just cannot live in this illness any longer."

When I opened my eyes, I saw I was bathed in light. Then from the middle of the light God sent a washing of love that penetrated every part of my being. As I stood in the light, it was as though I could see four-inch-tall letters that read, "YOU ARE HEALED."

Suddenly I found my hearing aid on my lap. For the first time I was able to hear without it. The noise in my head and the dizziness had vanished. Feeling in my extremities and head had returned. I could actually walk through a door without hitting the door frame. And taste! It came back in a little over a month, while I was licking envelopes in the office. That evening, as my daughter and I went up and down the aisles of the supermarket, I kept opening the packages as I threw them into the cart. I hadn't tasted food for four years and I couldn't wait!

I believe it is important, in the midst of a seemingly unanswered prayer, to *remember*. God clearly does respond—dramatically—to prayer. In our disappointment we may overlook what we have already received, the answers that have come, the "divine coincidences" that have accompanied so many requests.

Memory can therefore be an ally in the spiritual life. Recounting the blessings of the past gives us perspective on the present. Without memory of what God has already done, life may seem aimless. Prayer may seem like a futile enterprise.

In *The Man Who Mistook His Wife for a Hat*, neurologist Oliver Sacks recounts the story of a man, Mr. Thompson, whose memory had been obliterated by Korsakoff's syndrome. He would remember nothing for more than a few seconds, his loss of memory completely disorienting him. So he built bridges across the "abyss of amnesia" that opened continually beneath him by fluent confabulations and fictions of all kinds, one moment speaking as a delicatessen-grocer and the next as an imaginary reverend. Sacks theorizes that "to be ourselves we must *have* ourselves—possess, if need be repossess, our life-stories." Without remembering, life and prayer seem random, topsy-turvy.

Several years ago my family moved to a new community. Right up to the day of the move, and even beyond, we had little settled in terms of jobs or housing. Even though we had been unable to pull these vital elements together, my wife and I, supported by the wise counsel of friends, had a clear sense that we should move. During our preparations for the move I would sometimes read through pages of my journals from previous years just to be reminded that God had been faithful in the past. That helped me believe that God could be trusted for the present. Recalling those earlier answers helped me not lose my confidence that he was at work in my life.

That is why, I believe, the Bible speaks so often of memory. "I will remember the deeds of the Lord," said the psalmist, "yes, I will remember your miracles of long ago" (Psalm 77:11). Calling to mind God's prior faithfulness can be an antidote for spiritual depression. It keeps in perspective the seemingly unanswered prayer of the moment.

But some would say coming to terms with unanswered prayer is not quite so simple. A nineteen-year-old studying for the priesthood gets cancer, and a chorus of prayers arises. But he dies painfully, seemingly without sense, a promising life cut short. Or consider the evil of the Holocaust. Jewish theologian Martin Buber once asked, "Can one still speak to God after [the concentration camps of] . . . Auschwitz? Can one still, as an individual and as a people, enter at all into a dialogue relationship with Him? Dare we recommend to the survivors . . . the Jobs of the gas chambers, 'Call to Him, for He is kind, for His mercy endureth forever?' "[4]

The mystery of evil is great. There can be no glib answers to the achingly painful denials—the unanswered requests that leave us broken, devastated. When that happens, we have trouble even coming near God because of our disappointment.

Perhaps no one in the twentieth century has explained religious beliefs more winsomely and eloquently than Oxford don C. S. Lewis. Lewis, who lost his wife to cancer, wrestles with his grief in *A Grief Observed*: "Meanwhile, where is God? . . . [G]o to Him when your need is desperate, when all other help is vain, and what do you find? A door slammed in your face, and a sound of bolting and double bolting on the inside. After that, silence. . . . There are no lights in the windows. . . . It might be an empty house. Was it ever inhabited?"[5]

Is that the final word? When God refuses to intervene to save us from suffering, is that the defining moment of his relationship with us? Does he change from merciful Father to heartless rejecter?

Perhaps no one has asked such questions more poignantly than the Old Testament figure Job. He lost it all, you could say: his wife, family, possessions, health. He has become a symbol of affliction. But even in the midst of the heartache and unbelievable grief, to go away from God was unthinkable. God was still the center of Job's existence. So he said, "Though [God] slay me, yet will I hope in him" (Job 13:15). His experience with God, his memory of God's faithfulness, kept him from cursing God and giving up.

Job received no answers for his unanswered prayers. God brought not explanations, but *himself*. God, as the Bible said, "answered Job out of the storm" (Job 42:1). Not answers. But the Answer. The Presence. And that may be the only response we need.

One morning some years ago I was called out of a board meeting with an emergency call. A hospital in Santa Monica had called my wife with urgent news that my dad had been readmitted. He had had a severe heart attack just three weeks earlier, had partially recovered, and had been sent home. Indeed, I was scheduled to fly out the next day for a visit. But early that morning he had had another attack, and this time it looked like he could not survive longer than a few hours. I immediately hopped on a plane, hoping he would survive at least till I got there. I wanted to tell him one last time that I loved him. There had been a break between us some years earlier, and I felt there was still some finishing and resolving to be done. We had talked on the phone since his heart attack, of course, but I wanted to *see* him. And there had been no chance for him to put things in order, to tell me about the arrangements he had made for Mom, who was hopeless with anything financial. It seemed like a simple thing. So logical. So easy for God. "Please, Lord," I wrote in my journal not long before my plane landed, "keep Dad alive until I come."

I was greeted at the airport terminal by my mom and a friend of the family. It took but an instant to hear what I had dreaded: Dad had died even as I was winging my way home. My prayer was not answered.

But that is not what I remember most about that time. While I certainly shed tears, while I regretted missing seeing my father one last time, God answered me with his presence. He held me during a dark time.

The answer that matters more than any is knowing that we are not alone. That whatever the specific outcome, we can still know the promise of One who said, "Lo, I am with you always." We may never "solve" the mystery of evil. We may not receive the reprieve or healing or break we hoped for, but we can meet a presence who can carry us through the pain of what seems to be a meager answer. With him by our side, we find the ultimate Answer.

Prayers

Lord, I want not to storm your door and demand an answer. But I am anxious. I am waiting. If you will not bring what I'm asking for, please bring You. Amen.

> *May the Lord who is great and blessed look upon me,*
> *have pity on me and grant me peace.*
> *May he give me greater strength and courage*
> *that I may not be fearful or afraid.*
> *For the angels of God are about me*
> *and God is with me wherever I go.*

> —JEWISH PRAYER

11

Knowing What to Do
When Praying Seems
Impossible

O God . . . my soul thirsts for you, my body longs for you, in a dry and weary land where there is no water.

—PSALM 63:1

The profit and increase in spiritual life comes not only when you have devotion, but rather, when you can humbly and patiently bear the withdrawal and absence of devotion, yet not cease your prayers or leave undone your other customary good works.

—THOMAS À KEMPIS

On a hot summer day some years ago I went to the kitchen for a drink of water. But the faucet would only sputter. After a few spurts there was nothing. A drought had bled dry the underground spring that fed the pipes in our rural Virginia home. Suddenly I was really thirsty. Sweaty, dry-mouthed, I began craving what I could not have.

The discomfort and desperation that went along with my physical thirst finds a parallel in the spiritual life. Thirst is a powerful image for our desire for God, our need for replenishment within the dry depths of our spirits. Sometimes our life with God has the loamy moistness of a forest floor on a rainy day. We feel like a well-watered garden. But prayer can also feel like a desert. We try to pray but find we have nothing to say. Our souls resemble arid plains. Or we may be ready to talk, but it seems like God has gone into hiding. Or worse yet, that he has deserted us. At other times we sense God, but distractions war against our focus. Trying to pray becomes such a battle that we give it up.

More than we like to admit, prayer sometimes seems difficult and unrewarding. But that is precisely when we need to hang in there, to push past the obstacles.

When You Can't Concentrate

Often we sit down to pray and find our minds wandering. Distractions prove one of the most vexing problems in prayer. Perhaps the distraction is something simple—the teenage kid next door practicing electric guitar with window-rattling decibels, the couple in the apartment upstairs having another yelling binge. One day my morning run took me off the road into wilder, undeveloped land. I wound along a dirt path to a stand of trees. There the canopy of branches overhead and carpet of undergrowth below became a kind of sanctuary. I grew still and quiet. Unfortunately mosquitoes were also meditating there—and they soon discovered me. Their buzzing and biting quickly brought my spiritual reverie to a halt. "I throw myself down in my Chamber," wrote poet John Donne, "and I . . . invite God and his angels thither, and when they are there, I neglect God and his angels for the noise of a fly, for the rattling of a coach, for the whining of a door."[1]

At other times we are no sooner settled to pray in a quiet, still place than we think of something that "has to" get done. Or we can't stop wondering how our mortgage will get paid. Wandering thoughts usually have more to do with what is going on deep within than with interruptions from the outside. They have to do with our own cluttered inner closets.

Prayer reveals to us like few other things how unfocused our lives are. We are busied and worried by many things. The problem of scattered praying, then, requires more than devotional discipline. We need to examine our *lives*. What is the fundamental purpose of our living and striving? It is not that what we do is unimportant or useless. Nor does God expect us to withdraw from the civilized world. It is more a matter of clarifying the focus of our urgency, the center of our attention. When Jesus told his listeners to "seek first the kingdom of God," he was telling them (and us) that instead of worrying about the many things, we should concentrate on the one necessary thing. Our lives can be single, not scattered. Instead of playing to the crowd, we live for the Audience of One. When we settle that we are living for God, at least some of the distractions will fall away. We carry on our daily work with our purpose more sure, we go back to our praying with our reasons more defined.

Another reason distractions throw us off has to do with our worry about how prayer "feels." We measure its "effectiveness" by the minutes of concentrated focus. But our subjective impressions of our prayer times may not be correct. Indeed, a seemingly futile prayer time may be more significant than we know. "For this reason," argues spiritual writer Tad Dunne, "it is important to pay some attention to 'distractions' in prayer. They may be the real prayer, while the words we were mumbling are really distraction. A 'distraction' will be genuine prayer insofar as it arises out of a sufficiently deep sense of wonder about something in our experience. The 'prayer' may in reality be the distraction insofar as we use it to avoid facing life as it comes."[2]

So we carry on. We trust that below and behind our scattered processes a great unseen work is still being done. We pray by faith, not by sight. We believe that prayer matters even when we do not feel every moment comes wonderfully crystallized. God is more concerned about a heart that is turned toward him than about a mind that is neatly ordered and stoically calm.

This morning, like so many mornings, I sat down to pray. Wanting to let my wife sleep in, I soon had on my hands a very awake five-year-old yelling for maple "oartmeal." Once I had Bekah settled with bowl and spoon, I slipped off to another room, Bible, journal, and prayer list in hand. I managed a few moments of prayer before she found me. I enjoyed having her snuggle against me while she watched TV, but a time of uninterrupted peace it was not. And even when I was alone, I had trouble getting my mind off yesterday's projects at work. I had trouble concentrating. And yet I prayed. While I would not memorialize it as a watershed of charged spiritual passion, real prayer took place. God was pleased. My effort was not in vain.

It is said that once Martin Luther's dog happened to be near the table, and the dog noticed with open mouth what Luther was eating. Luther commented, "Oh, if I could only pray the way this dog watches the meat! All his thoughts are concentrated on the piece of meat. Otherwise he has no thought, wish, or hope." We *can* get better at concentrating. Progress is possible. While we are always beginners in prayer, we can form new habits. We can establish new "grooves." Our minds and bodies are wonderfully designed to respond to exercise and discipline. Just as our biceps and calf muscles grow stronger with exertion, so can our spiritual faculties.

Which means we can take advantage of some practical ways to minimize the distraction of distractions.

• *Get up early in the morning (or stay up late at night).* Usually you can beat the rest of the household (at least the kids) by setting your alarm a little early. A mere fifteen minutes in the living room to gather your thoughts and pray can make a difference in any day.

• *Keep your praying simple.* I have spoken elsewhere on centering prayer (the repeated use of a single word or brief phrase to help our minds gain focus). Meditatively, slowly reciting a memorized prayer such as the Lord's Prayer can help (more on this in the following chapter). Or begin with simply stating that you want to talk to God and be in loving relationship to him. Remembering that prayer is ultimately about *God* and not forms or formulas can give your prayer a spaciousness that allows you to rise above the frantic pace of your harried mind.

• *Vary the routine.* There is no reason to lock in a pre-scribed pattern if a change of pace occasionally helps you not get bored or distracted. Writer and journalist Tim Bascom tells of how for a time he got tired of "praying in the usual way every night." So for a year or so he and his wife would sing a hymn every night. "We kept a hymnbook by our bed. We would pick a hymn, sometimes one that seemed especially to fit what we were experiencing, and sing it as a prayer." We need not worry about there being only one "right" way to pray.

When Praying Seems Uneven

Because prayer is largely about a relationship, because it has so much to do with intangibles such as desire and faith, we sometimes like to think that no work or discipline will be necessary. We prefer spontaneity. And there are those times when something wonderful just "happens." The words come to us. The longing for God rises with no coaxing. Praying seems effortless.

But no relationship can be built solely on impromptu utterances. There needs to be diligence. Sometimes we must work. "The only way to pray is to pray," writes spiritual teacher Dom John Chapman, "and the way to pray well is to pray much. If one has no time for this, then one must at least pray regularly. But the less one prays, the worse it goes. And if circumstances do not permit even regularity, then one must put up with the fact that when one does try to pray, one can't pray—and our prayer will probably consist of telling this to God."[3] We cannot get by without some constancy and consistency.

My friend Julie Parham's job involves relating to high-profile book publishers and movie agents, leading a life she describes as "incredibly hectic." "Prayer for me," she tells me, "must be more than spontaneous: I must make it a habit, almost a ritual like brushing my teeth. I do it whether I like to or not. I have made progress only from continued, habitual prayer."

So sometimes I find that I raise myself out of bed in the mornings to pray whether I *feel* like it or not. I try to read the Bible—a psalm plus another chapter or two—whether it is my first choice of reading matter or not. Periodically we all need to stand back from the filigree of our daily schedules and look at the broad strokes and overall composition. I believe that every life will benefit from a regular cycle of Bible reading. I believe most people should schedule regular time for prayer. Disciplines such as keeping a prayer journal and reading the insights of spiritual writers may also help. The "big picture" settled, we carry out the particulars whether feelings always follow or not.

Following other disciplines helps untie us from our attachment to the many "things" of our lives. Fasting, the conscious decision to do without food for, say, a morning or a day, can help us focus on God. It can free us from our temptation to give food and its pleasure too much power. Or, taking seriously the admonition of the Bible not to "give up meeting together," we can resolve to attend religious services every week and observe the day as a fast from work.

There is another side to all this, of course. Thinking about discipline sometimes leaves us uneasy. For one thing we know our track record is mixed, as the countless exercise bikes gathering dust in garages across the country testify. Our plans to pray more regularly go the way of New Year's resolutions or the latest fad diet. We start and stop often.

Or disciplines can become legalisms. Rather than providing simple form and structure, our exercises stifle. They become a burden. We become weighed down, even fearful of not following through. We can become wedded to our programs, convinced that true spirituality will come with just one more technique, one more sacrifice. We forget that practices should always be seen as means, not ends. The aim is not to rack up points for heroic effort but to be closer to God.

I don't consider myself exceptionally disciplined. I recognize the value of exercise and I run some mornings, but I never log my running times and miles. I run four times one week and one time the next. I know I should read the classics

of literature, but I have started (but not finished) Dosto-
yevsky's *The Brothers Karamazov* more times than I like to
admit. And I find it much the same when it comes to prayer.

So it's not surprising that I have failed at some of my
more ambitious attempts. Reading one man's commitment to
pray an hour every day, for example, once inspired me to do
the same—for about two weeks. I appreciate those who organize their devotions with Day-Timers and checklists. I've
tried with my share of alarm-blasting mornings to do the
same. And while I keep a spiritual journal to record what I
think God says to me, the frequency seems erratic. I have
come to believe that some of us will never be zealously orga-
nized and wonderfully disciplined in our praying because we
don't approach any aspect of our lives that way. Our tem-
peraments are different.

A friend of mine confessed, "I simply have not been able
to become more disciplined about some kind of regimented
schedule." But, she continued, "I don't think I'm falling ter-
ribly short on this. I talk to God in the midst of anything and
everything, whether for a passing moment in the midst of
doing the laundry, giving a speech, or actually kneeling in
prayer."

One man came up to author Steve Brown and said he
needed help with developing a regular prayer life:

> "I really want to have that time, but I've tried to start
> and have quit even more times than I've tried to quit
> smoking. Can you help me?"
> I told him that . . . in his enthusiasm for having a

time of prayer, he was overcommitting himself. I suggested that he take no more than five or ten minutes each morning to read a passage of Scripture, to spend some time telling God how wonderful he is and thanking him for all he has done, to confess all the sins he could remember, to pray the Lord's Prayer, and to pray about the things that bothered him. "Then quit," I said. "Don't increase the time you spend until it is absolutely necessary that you increase it. Don't go beyond the ten minutes until you simply can't stay within the ten minutes." That simple advice absolutely changed his talk with God. Now he can accurately be described as a man of prayer.[4]

It may not be easy, but it gets easier. We establish some habits that become familiar. We gain a certain pleasure from the predictability. Not long ago I had a week where I began each morning with a half-hour run. I had gotten submerged in so much busyness in the weeks before that I had had little exercise. I was out of shape. And that first day when I ran, my body dragged. I wanted to be somewhere else, doing anything but picking up my heavy feet, pushing my tired body, taxing my reluctant lungs.

But I noticed something as the week progressed. The running became more natural, less of an effort. I started to look forward to each run.

Around the same time, a friend shared an insight he got from a conference on the spiritual life. Becoming more disciplined in your prayer life will feel at first like you're swimming upstream. It will be hard work. But if you keep at it, someday, suddenly the current will reverse directions—and it will carry you along, if you let it.

When Prayer Seems Dry

No matter how rich and full our praying may seem as we begin, most people move into feelingless, arid stretches. "In the beginning" of his times in God's presence, writes Rick, a forty-three-year-old mental health therapist, "I was surprised to be deeply 'touched' emotionally at the beginning of each [prayer] session. This seemed a sign that something was happening for me. I was spurred on by the results." But in recent months that has changed. "There are no feelings other than intermittent impatience with being in a place that feels barren."

Those who take prayer seriously commonly go through a period, sometimes a long period, when they experience the apparent absence of God. The warm flush of feelings vanishes.

This may be tied, first of all, to barrenness in our emotional lives. When nerves fray and calm unravels, prayer sometimes comes harder. The loss of a child, the pain of a divorce, a diagnosis of serious illness: These things can so shatter our composure that we find all of our routines upset.

More commonly, I believe, bouts of dryness have to do with spiritual dynamics. The ways we have previously thought about God suddenly seem shallow. We undergo a purifying of our conceptions of God. But as we are letting go of the old ways of seeing him, after perhaps fashioning him in our own image, the God we knew seems absent or even non-existent. It feels like we are "beating on Heaven's door with bruised knuckles in the dark," to use pastor and writer George Buttrick's phrase.[5] Whether we name it a spiritual dry spell or a "dark night of the soul," the results can be startling and discouraging. A person may even begin to doubt his or her faith.

Ironically such times may actually be a sign of deepening faith. They mean that the soul is seeking for a more genuine knowledge of God. We are letting go of the superficial faith that got us by for a while. And while something deeper and more profound is growing in its place, the *sensation* is barrenness. The letting go of the familiar creates pain. God is withering up our confidence in our old ways of relating. Or perhaps God withdraws the sense of his presence so that we can recognize its sweetness when it returns.

How do we make our way through such times? One way is simply not to give up. We carry on. I was impressed by the way my friend Cathy Kelly coped: "Even in the dry, desert experience of this past summer I would take the time that was 'designated' as prayer time and at least 'show up.' Maybe all I did was sit, but I found that the sitting itself was prayer, that the important part was that I set aside the time to be in total attentiveness to God."

Or sometimes you can try to make the dryness a prayer in itself by acknowledging it before God. You offer it to God. You can try to remember that, as contemplative writer Thomas Merton notes, "There is no such thing as a prayer in which 'nothing is done' or 'nothing happens,' although there may well be a prayer in which nothing is perceived or felt or thought."[6] You don't have to feel spiritually together for prayer to matter.

Dotty Biros, a middle-aged midwesterner, tells of a particularly stressful time in her marriage. "I was hurting so bad, things in my life were so crazy, I couldn't pray. I didn't know what to ask for. I felt so alone. So some nights I just sang the child's song 'Jesus Loves Me.' It was such a simple song, but I could sing that until I fell asleep. I knew God would honor that. The least little bit, he'll honor that."[7]

So we slog through. And as we do, we recall that we are not alone, even if we feel so. We pray in the faith that God not only hears our dry prayers, he helps us through them:

> Blessed is the man who trusts in the Lord,
>   whose confidence is in him.
> He will be like a tree planted by the water
>   that sends out its roots by the stream.
> It does not fear when heat comes;
>   its leaves are always green.
> It has no worries in a year of drought
>   and never fails to bear fruit. (Jeremiah 17:7–8)

When We Feel Harassed

I should end with a caution: We occasionally encounter in prayer (and in life) something even more unsettling than dryness. We face times for which mere persistence will not be sufficient. During such times we gain glimpses that we are engaged in a fierce battle for which nothing less than supernatural resources will do.

Rob Wheeler is a twenty-something southerner who works at a computer-printer manufacturer. During his freshman year of college he experienced wonderful growth in his faith. He loved to pray, so much so that he sometimes had trouble waiting for class to be done so that he could get back to his room to pray.

But one day, he recounts, "I rested my head on my desk to close my eyes and pray. Immediately it was as though I was looking down a dark tunnel. I could 'see' threatening faces, and heard, in my imagination, eerie, screaming voices. It was like a horror movie."

The hideous images continued for several hours, every time he closed his eyes to pray. "It was so obvious it was a spiritual attack," he says. "I felt that demons were trying to keep me from praying. Finally, as I claimed that Christ had authority, the images stopped. I felt peace. I could go to bed and actually sleep."

His story may seem extreme, but it reminds me that prayer cannot always be gentle and calm. Sometimes it is a battle. Sometimes Sunday-school prayers of the Jesus-meek-and-mild variety are not enough. We should not hesitate to pray militantly, boldly, whenever we see ourselves or someone else harassed by the demonic. This explains why the biblical writers and other spiritual mentors sometimes make use of the images of war when describing our spiritual work. "Put on the full armor of God, so that you can take your stand against the devil's schemes," wrote Paul the apostle (Ephesians 6:11).

Evil not only exists, it works with persuasive and intensely personal power. For centuries spiritual writers have seen demons as more than metaphor, the devil more than symbol. All that inhabits the spiritual realm is not pure and good. In prayer we face off against spiritual forces malign in intention. "Anyone who has ever tried to formulate a private prayer in silence, and in his own heart," writes David Bolt, "will know what I mean by diabolical interference. The forces of evil are in opposition to the will of God. And the nearer a person approaches God's will, the more apparent and stronger and more formidable this opposition is seen to be. It is only when we are going in more or less the same direction as the devil that we are unconscious of any opposition at all."[8]

Evil taunts us with a seductive voice and oily reasoning. It arises within us, yet we also know it as a force outside of us. When Jesus began his ministry, he was led into a wilderness to be tempted by the devil. He was harassed by a malevolence that wielded ingenious subtlety and persistent logic. When Jesus sent his followers out preaching and healing, it was with the warning that they would be "lambs in the midst of wolves." Peter, one of Jesus' first followers, later cautioned an early church, "Your enemy the devil prowls around like a roaring lion looking for someone to devour."

The supernatural realm warrants care and discernment, lest we sweep out the clutter in our inner lives only to have it reoccupied by that which is even worse. Even Satan can masquerade as an angel of light, the Bible tells us.

We should not be alarmed when prayer requires our donning the armor of faith, or calling out to God in Jesus' name for the power of the Holy Spirit. To talk of the devil not only explains our experience, it exposes our enemy. So we need not delay in calling on God's limitless power when we "pray against" temptation in all its many varieties: addiction, lust, greed, deception—all that would enslave and destroy what God created to be free and holy. We pray, "Lord, in Jesus' powerful name, we invite your presence to be here." And we turn to Scripture: "for the word of God is living and active. Sharper than any double-edged sword, it penetrates even to dividing soul and spirit, joints and marrow; it judges the thoughts and attitudes of the heart" (Hebrews 4:12). We find promises there of God's vanquishing power over evil and the demonic and we live and pray in the confidence they bring.

I also believe that if throughout our praying our goal remains to look to God and think of him, we need not worry. God has disarmed the demonic powers. God can be trusted to be our strength. God can drive out that which would plague our thoughts or poison our praying. After telling the early church to "test the spirits to see whether they are from God," the writer of the New Testament letter called 1 John reminds his hearers, "You . . . are from God and have overcome them, because the one who is in you is greater than the one who is in the world" (1 John 4:1–4). The Crucifixion and the Resurrection of Jesus show that God is victorious over the forces of evil and death. And that is a victory in which we can share.

Prayers

Why, O Lord, is it so hard for me to keep my heart directed toward you? Why do the many little things I want to do, and the many people I know, keep crowding my mind, even during the hours that I am totally free to be with you and you alone? . . . Do I keep wondering, in the center of my being, whether you will give me all I need if I just keep my eyes on you?

Please accept my distractions, my fatigue, my irritations, and my faithless wanderings. You know me more deeply and fully than I know myself. You love me with a greater love than I can love myself. You even offer me more than I desire. Look at me, see me in all my misery and inner confusion, and let me sense your presence in the midst of my turmoil.

—HENRI NOUWEN[9]

Lord, I thank you for your great power made vivid in Jesus. May his love keep me on the straight path and his strength make me safe from all harm. Amen.

12

Seeking Out Model Prayers

The child learns to speak because his father speaks to him. . . . So we learn to speak to God because God has spoken to us and speaks to us. By means of the speech of his Father in heaven his children learn to speak to him. Repeating God's words after him, we begin to pray to him.

—DIETRICH BONHOEFFER

My son Micah is learning to play the piano. He's good. But sometimes he complains about the scales and arpeggios and cadences. They seem like drudgery. And reading a new piece of music is usually not as much fun as playing around with blues runs. So I tell him, "Go ahead and improvise." But not all the time. Making up riffs as he goes has its limits. His fingers need the dexterity that comes from repetition. Certain techniques will come only with long hours of lessons and practice. And when he tires of his own experimenting, the quarter rests and eighth notes his teacher drills into him will open up a world of music.

That we are made to pray does not mean we never need "practice." Sometimes we need to do more than improvise. Our prayers need sound instruction. When I run low on words, I need the kind of grounding in good habits that Micah's piano lessons give him. I need teachers. I need to spend time with the prayers of others until I get them right. Then my own prayers will have greater fluency and depth.

Jesus' disciples came to their teacher and said, "Teach us to pray." They might as well have been speaking for us—for me. I need help with my fumbling words and sometimes awkward silences. I don't want to make prayer an exercise in rote woodenness, but I also know I need a model or pattern when words don't exactly roll off the tongue. I don't want always to have to figure out my prayers from scratch.

Fortunately I can find help from a host of possibilities.

In the long history of faithful spiritual teachers, for example, not only do we find teaching *about* prayer, we see real people *praying*. So we can take "notes." We observe the words they used and the way they used them. We let our words fall into rhythm with theirs. We watch for the choirmaster's cues. We mimic the painter's strokes. If imitation is a form of flattery, it is also a wonderful way to learn. Some people, of course, find the very idea of written or read prayers off-putting, akin, as Richard Foster puts it, "to meeting an old friend on the street and quickly thumbing through a textbook to find an appropriate greeting."[1] But my collections of the prayers of others sometimes help me. I don't always want to come up with the words. I need to be stretched sometimes by the good insights of wiser pray-ers.

And with Scripture's prayers we can start with the prayers that others have used and proved before us, each word, as Eugene Peterson writes, "carrying the experience of generations."[2] Even better, by praying Scripture, God's revealed Word, we are praying after God's very words.

Indeed one of the most transforming insights for my praying came with the discovery that Scripture could not only be read, it could be also *prayed*. I began to approach the Bible as a prayer book. I prayed using the actual words. I watched Jesus model an astounding familiarity with God, calling God *Abba* (Aramaic for "Daddy"). Emboldened by him, I did too. Or I read Paul's words to the Ephesians in the New Testament, about his prayer that God would give his listeners "the Spirit of wisdom and revelation, so that [they] may know him better." I saw him asking that the "eyes of [their] hearts may be enlightened in order that [they] may know the hope to which he has called [them], the riches of his glorious inheritance." I began to take such passages and fill in the names of friends, or even use them in prayers for myself. Through repeating God's words after him, I had the feeling of an eager, devoted child who learns to speak through imitation. And I had the feeling that I was praying not only at God's invitation but with his coaching. It gave me new confidence.

I also learned about "praying the promises." When God,

speaking through the biblical writers and characters, promised some good thing or declared some immutable blessing, I took him at his word. I came to God saying, "This is what you promised." My prayers started with what I already knew God wanted to do.

Then I discovered the Bible's collection of psalms. I started rummaging around in all 150 poems and promises and worship choruses. Many of the psalms are in fact explicit prayers. The whole collection, called the Psalter, carries with it the inflections and rhythms of praise, worship, anguish, anger, hope, confession, and shame. It is, in other words, patently true to life. My life. In the thick of day-to-day living, to be able to call to mind a snatch of the Psalms— "[Your] steadfast love endures forever," or "Lord, you have been our dwelling place throughout all generations"—made all the difference in how I moved through an anxious time. Many mornings, as I sat down aware of the time and of my need to get going, I would open to a psalm and find myself slowing down, praying something I never would have thought of. I understand why Martin Luther said centuries ago of others' ways of praying, "Ah, there is not the juice, the strength, the passion, the fire which I find in the Psalter."

Memorizing Scripture is also helping me pray. It allows God's Word to bring form and beauty to my own sometimes artless praying. Waiting in line at a checkout line or trying to go to sleep at night can become opportunities to think about the promises of God, to mold my thoughts around his truths. The passages we select need not be lengthy; indeed, it is best if they are not. Right now I am memorizing John 14:21, where Jesus says, "Whoever has my commands and obeys them, he is the one who loves me. He who loves me will be loved by my Father, and I too will love him and show myself to him." As I memorize and recite, I try to pray my way into the meaning, and let the words suggest prayers, such as "Help me, Lord, obey you" or "Show yourself to me, God."

That we can pray God's own words after him is especially true of the Lord's Prayer, or, as it is known in some traditions, the Our Father. Found in Luke 11, this prayer that Jesus gave his followers when they asked him to teach them to pray must be the most often-quoted prayer in the Bible. And with good reason. Here Jesus touches the great themes of praying: praise, confession, and petition. When we begin to plumb its depths, we will discover it as far more than a hastily recited, rote prayer done as pure ritual.

The petitions of the Lord's Prayer, I find, can give my longings focus, helping me to think through the issues and urgencies of the day. Someone once asked a nineteenth-century spiritual teacher about cultivating a deeper prayer life. She is said to have replied, "Say the Lord's Prayer, but take an hour to say it." Here is how, as recorded in one of my recent journal entries, I allowed this model prayer to guide me through a rich morning prayer time:

> *Our Father in heaven*   It's good to know you are in "heaven," Lord, that whatever else that means, you are above the push and pull of my little world. That you are aware of all that happens in the world around me.

Hallowed be your name   Lord, you are to be revered. Even your name is sacred. Help me to hallow it—treating it as holy and sacred.

Your kingdom come   All the goodness and mercy and strength that make up your rule on earth, Lord, help that come into being.

Your will be done   May your plans not be thwarted by others. May your purposes find no obstacle in me. I want to be willing.

On earth, as it is in heaven   I pray that my actions will more closely resemble your heavenly designs.

Give us this day our daily bread   Lord, you know my family's need for food, for shelter, for transportation. Help me not to forget how my job helps provide for our daily needs. And help me always depend first on you and on your generosity.

Forgive us our trespasses, as we forgive those who trespass against us   Lord, I need your forgiveness. I admit that I get caught up in stresses and pressures, that I do not always keep my focus on you. And I have been cranky with my family. Forgive me. And help me to forgive my friend Anna, who hurt me needlessly.

Lead us not into temptation   Help me make choices for the good today.

But deliver us from evil   I count on your help! I need your Holy Spirit's power to save me from myself.

For thine is the kingdom, and the power, and the glory, forever.   Lord, it means so much to serve such a gracious God, who holds the world in his hands!

I find such a guide helpful when I am lying in bed, unable to sleep at night or get up in the morning. Or when I find my mind wandering. Or when my self-made prayers seem to grind into a rut. "To this day," sixteenth-century spiritual leader Martin Luther once said, "I am still nursing myself on the Lord's Prayer like a child and am still eating and drinking of it like an old man without getting bored with it." And we need not pray the whole prayer through each time. It sometimes happens that I get so caught up in one of the petitions that I forgo the others. Many are the times I have not gotten farther than "Our Father in heaven."

The ways to give shape to our longing to converse with God are many. Prayer books, such as the Episcopal *Book of Common Prayer*, provide a wealth of raw material for praying. Many have suggested prayers for morning and evening, for the church seasons, even for times of birth or death. Some prayer books are focused on particular themes, such as motherhood or college graduation. Others collect hundreds of prayers from across the centuries and cultures. Daily devotional guides or prayer calendars often help us pray as well.

I like to experiment with these myriad ways of praying. Sometimes I take time with the printed prayer of another until

I make it my own. Hearing others pray aloud often gives me cues. For a period of some weeks I found the Lord's Prayer the most helpful basis for praying, using it with emphasis on praise and intercessory prayer for others. Other weeks I use a monthly cycle of psalms (such as is found in the Episcopal *Book of Common Prayer*). Or for a time I will read through a chapter of Scripture a day, trying not only to assimilate what happened, but to understand the passage's relevance for the day's prayers.

The assumption that prayer is only what we do when we are by ourselves, the lonely soul before God, may limit our prayers as much as an insistence on always "making them up." We live in an individualistic age, where the assumption is that a lonely walk in the woods is better for the soul than a meeting with other believers.

But left to myself, my prayers become imbalanced or stuck at an elementary stage. I need a way to avoid letting the eccentricities of my personal faith take me too far off track. I also tend to get bogged down in my emotions. And feelings, as professor of spiritual theology Eugene Peterson notes, can be the "scourge of prayer. To pray by feelings is to be at the mercy of glands and weather and indigestion. And there is no mercy in any of them."[3] My moods are too fickle to be reliable guides for all of my spiritual life. And besides, there is a world of reality that I am too small to see by myself. I need the expanding of vision that praying with others brings. Prayer needs the soil of community to put down roots and flourish.

So when I come to worship in a blue funk, it does me

good to join in a congregation's choruses of alleluias. Or I may be feeling cocky, convinced all is well with me and the world. I need the reminder of prayers of confession that I still stumble and desperately need God's forgiveness. Perhaps I am complacent, living as I do in a comfortable house and a pleasant neighborhood. I need to be called to intercession for the world's hungry and poor.

And when I feel spiritually dry, when I don't feel particularly fluent or spiritual, I can be carried along by the momentum of the worship service. My words can find new footing. There is great comfort sometimes in "being led" in prayer. Someone stands in front of us and helps our untold longings find expression. Suddenly it is not up to just us. Our egos are no longer front and center. The corporate focus of worship—God—is. Liturgy, the technical word for the way churches order their worship, is, as priest and author Simon Tugwell writes, "essentially something given, and in this it expresses a fundamental feature of all prayer. Its sublime lack of concern for our personal moods is a forcible reminder that when we come to God, it is not to force our moods or our interests on to him, but to receive his interests and to let him, in a sense, share his moods with us."[4]

Perhaps it is no accident that much of the corporate prayer of synagogue and church through the centuries has incorporated music. Song brings our prayers into rhythm and harmony with others. It reminds us that we need others to make a chorus. Our lonely voice does not a congregation make.

And we need each other's voices, each other's prayers, each other's presence to make a go of prayer.

I suppose that Micah could learn a certain amount of piano on his own, just as I could pull together some kind of makeshift spiritual life as a hermit. But I know he would never go far. He needs the weekly prodding and encouragement of his teacher, Mrs. Williams. He needs her to pick out the songs and listen until he gets them right. And when his groping hits an impasse, I know she will take him to the next level.

I'll remember that the next time I think I can get by for long without others.

Prayers

May my lips overflow with praise,
*   for you teach me your decrees.*
May my tongue sing of your word,
*   for all your commands are righteous.*
I long for your salvation, O Lord,
*   and your law is my delight.*

—*PSALM 119:171–74*

Speak, Lord, for your servant hears.
Grant us ears to hear,
Eyes to see,
Wills to obey,
Hearts to love.

—*CHRISTINA ROSSETTI (NINETEENTH CENTURY)*[5]

13

Finding That Two Are
Better Than One

A soul which remains alone . . . is like a burning coal
which is left by itself: It will grow colder rather than hotter.

—JOHN OF THE CROSS

If two lie down together, they will keep warm.
But how can one keep warm alone?

—ECCLESIASTES 4:9–11

Several years ago a friend invited me to join him for a hike in
a bird and wildlife sanctuary on the Gulf Coast of Texas. At
first, as we walked the gravel road that crisscrossed the
marshland of the refuge, I saw only clear sky, clumps of dry
reeds, and a few ducks.

I wasn't impressed.

But my friend Merle knew birds. "Look—there!" he would say, pointing to the sweeping wings of a great blue heron in flight or a soaring black-shouldered kite. With the help of his sharp eye and binoculars, I soon glimpsed roseate spoonbills with broad beaks and bony legs preening in a distant pond. Merle pointed out every kind of duck imaginable, more than I could ever name or now remember. Once he cocked his ear and had me listen for the rasping, eerie call of grackles perched nearby. With him along, a new world opened to my senses.

Experiences like these remind me that I cannot live well without help. All of us have had friends, mentors, or guides whose influence lives on inside us. Here or there a parent, aunt, schoolteacher, or neighbor has left an indelible mark on our souls. We could not go far without them, without their presence or insight or encouragement or tough word.

It is the same with prayer.

Through the years I have found other *people* indispensable to my growth in praying. They have helped me see glimmers of God's presence I would have overlooked when left to my own devices. They have shown me new angles on what God was doing in my life. They have reminded me to listen to God's truth when I grew complacent or full of myself. Sometimes they have simply stood by me when I knew I should pray but didn't feel like it.

While much of this book has focused on individual, personal prayer, I would be remiss if I did not say that prayer is very much a corporate enterprise. It is preeminently done in the company of others. Prayer takes place on many a lonely hillside or empty church building of course, but even more where, as Jesus said, "two or three are gathered" in his name. The road to spiritual maturity is more easily traveled with another spiritual pilgrim. Our praying can go only so far if we do not join it with the longing chorus of a worshiping congregation.

Knowing that we need other people to pray well, however, leaves us with mixed feelings. We have much to overcome before we turn to others. Our culture's love of rugged individualism has so infected our praying that we hesitate. Prayer for many of us still seems like a private enterprise. "We would prefer," writes Eugene Peterson, "to stand tall and alone in our prayers."[1] But "doing it my way" is no mark of heroism when it comes to the spiritual life. Rugged individualism, which whispers to us that only the weak need others, is a peculiarly American heresy. Spirituality is not a do-it-yourself project. We were made for others in life and love, and we were made to be with others when we pray. So we turn now to look at the communal dimension of prayer. How can the presence and insights of others help us in our praying?

We Can Expect to Find Immense Support from the Simple Presence of Others Who Share Our Spiritual Hunger

Knowing I do not face the battles of daily life and spiritual growth alone matters a great deal.

For a number of years, until a move to another state brought things to a halt, I met for an hour a week, over lunch, with a colleague and friend. We saw ourselves as "mutual mentors." And while the topics of our conversations ranged far and wide, much of what we were about was spiritual growth. He had no license in counseling, I no official certification in "spiritual direction," but we brought to each other a simple willingness to listen to the other's joys and struggles and, toward the end of each hour, to pray out loud for each other.

We find such mutual support in many settings. Public worship services, house-church meetings, twelve-step recovery groups, and Sunday-school classes can all provide an opportunity to know that when we kneel or stand or bow before God, our bent knees and lifted hands and lowered heads are part of a larger whole. We realize we are not alone when we voice our laments or praises or supplications. We become part of a mighty army.

We Can Expect Others to Help Us Make Holy Sense of Everyday Life

I am sometimes tempted to think that my anxiety about paying the bills or being a good father to three children has little to do with more "lofty" concerns. But I have come to see that from the moment the alarm jars me awake in the morning until the house grows quiet at night, God is at work in my life—in the dramatic *and* in the ordinary. Spiritual mentors and companions can help me remember to stay alert and open-eyed.

Once a friend and colleague stung me with what I'm sure he felt was helpful honesty. He told me he found me "naive." I was confused and hurt. When my friend and mutual mentor, Kevin, and I got together, I shared what had happened. I knew I needed another perspective, a second opinion, to help me sort through what was true insight and what was simply insult. Kevin listened prayerfully, prayed out loud for me, and gave perspective. "I think you should basically ignore the criticism," he said. "I know you, and I think what he is putting you down for is really a God-given simplicity. Don't let go of that." I was able to move through a difficult experience with not only personal support but with spiritual perspective on a troubling experience.

And sometimes I am liable not so much to miss what God is saying as to misread it. How spiritual some of my ambitions sometimes seem! And how theologically correct my excuses for not doing good. Until, that is, another voice, a minister or neighbor or spouse committed to the same path, has the courage to point out my mixed motives. When my schedule crowds out time for exercise, or family relationships, or prayer, I need someone to remind me that the tasks that seem so urgent may not be worth the compromise. I need others to ensure that my spiritual life does not become an exercise in spiritual self-indulgence.

We Can Expect the Insights of Other Believers to Help Keep Our Praying on Track

Prayer does not automatically confer goodness. It does not even guarantee we will move ever closer to truth. It is possible to pray in a way that drives us only farther into pride and self-absorption. Praying can even reinforce our error and arrogance. And because when we pray, we tend to see ourselves as more spiritual, it can leave us all the more impervious to correction. Wise spiritual masters know that our own opinions are deceptive guides. "He becomes the disciple of a fool," wrote Bernard of Clairvaux in the twelfth century, "who sets himself up to be his own teacher." Left only to ourselves, we can bend and distort and remake prayer into something that serves our hankerings for self-indulgence. "No one can walk without a guide," wrote Augustine centuries before Bernard. Whatever the age we live in, to truly grow in prayer requires some unlearning and leaving behind.

Indeed, in the spiritual realm we will come across paths that, while attractive at first glance, are not only unhelpful but also dangerous. If, as the Bible says, Satan himself can masquerade as an angel of light, we dare not be smug. We do well not to insist that we can always figure things out on our own. Evil almost never looks nefarious at first glance. It is too seductive. We need the trusted wisdom of theologically sound teachers and guides not given to flying after the trendy or silly or shallow. We need companions soaked in the wisdom of Scripture, focused on Christ, rooted in the tradition of spiritual wisdom. Which is why the revealed truth of Scripture, sometimes in the words of another human person, is so essential. To pray, in other words, requires us to find guidance from others.

Of course any group, even one specifically assembled to nurture spiritual growth, can itself become ingrown and prey to spiritual eccentricity. Many of the heresies and horrors of the church's history started among inspired compatriots. "Sometimes," writes Eugene Peterson, "a group diminishes us: we are leveled down, lumped into the less-than-average, and become less than ourselves."[2] We can be lead astray by others of course, not just by our own hearts.

But so much can happen when we tap into the communal wisdom and enabling energies of a group. We are more likely to stay focused on truth if we keep our growth in fluency in talking to God a cooperative venture. "As iron sharpens iron," the proverb goes, "so one [person] sharpens another" (Proverbs 27:17). How often I have felt myself growing sluggish in devotion only to have my passion rekindled by a sermon or a worship service or a simple word of encouragement from another.

Over the years I have discerned within myself a tendency toward perfectionism. My striving always to do everything "just so" has not only brought extra pressures to my relationships, it has colored my image of God. When I once bemoaned my failure to be more regular in prayer, my spiritual mentor at the time gently suggested that I was perhaps too hard on myself when it came to prayer, that I needed to relax more in God's presence and simply to enjoy him.

As comforting and reassuring as her message could have been, I resisted. I preferred to see myself as a spiritual athlete, frustrated but determined in my pursuit of devotional heroics. But when, just a short time later, another friend suggested that I needed to rest more in God's promise of acceptance, to receive what God wanted to do in me as a gift, not a merit badge, it became increasingly difficult for me to deny what my mentor was saying. For all my protests, those remarks helped bring balance to my prayer life.

A fellowship or friend can also shed light on the content of our praying. We may get bogged down in one way or pattern. Perhaps we always concentrate on answers to personal, daily needs. Or perhaps we *never* do. As we have seen, our devotional life needs a wide range of praise to God, confession of sin, intercession for ourselves and others, and thanksgiving for blessings received. We need times of talking to God, but also stretches of restful listening. Another person "listening in" on our praying or reminding us in a teaching of the rudiments, may steer us back again.

Turning to Another Can Help Us When We Need to Confess

While I believe that we need no mediator between us and God save his Son, sometimes others can embody God's forgiveness. We may benefit by hearing God's pardon on the lips of another.

I am fascinated by research that shows that unburdening ourselves of painful memories or guilty secrets may significantly improve our physical health. Researcher James Pennebaker demonstrated measurable physiological differences in people who confessed wrongs or talked about disturbing personal episodes compared with those who never divulged their dark secrets. In one study college students who had unburdened themselves needed measurably fewer visits to the college infirmary. The difference seemed related not to any specific counsel given in response, but rather to the simple act of bringing out into the open what had been hidden.[3]

Confessors can do us good, which may be why for centuries Indians of North and South America have had elaborate confession rituals wherein tribe members disclosed their wrongdoing to others. And why some churches formalize a process by which a person confesses his or her sins to a priest or minister. Whatever the form, the idea is not to carry our burdens alone.

Participation in a Community of Faith and Belief Helps Us Ground Our Spiritual Lives in Something More Solid Than Opinions or Feelings

If we wait only for personal inspiration, our praying will be erratic. But when we are in dry spells, we may find that

during these times we grow in prayer only through the structure of weekly worship, through the challenges of a group
that holds us accountable, or through the honesty of a friend
who demands from us the best when we are tempted to offer
only yesterday's leftovers.

When we pray, we often do so because something inside
us prompts it. But we often pray not only because our feelings
nudge us but because we are part of a larger whole. When we
worship with others, it is not *our* experience that precipitates
prayer. We are freed from the incessant need always to have
to figure out what to say, or for how long, or in what tone of
voice. Someone else, vested with the authority (formal or
otherwise) of centuries-old tradition, gives us guidance,
jump-starts our efforts to reach out to God, even provides us
the mold into which our words can comfortably, gently fit.
We allow ourselves to relax and be led. We don't have to
perform. We allow our own prayers, stumbling and faltering
as they may sometimes be, to be carried along by something
that needs little or nothing of us. "Two are better than one,"
I read in Ecclesiastes,

> because they have good return for their work:
> If one falls down,
>   his friend can help him up.
> But pity the man who falls
>   and has no one to help him up! (4:9–10)

Prayer

Lord, I'm tempted sometimes to go inside myself. I think I can make my spiritual life a do-it-yourself project. But you have said in your Word that two are better than one, that Jesus is present where two or three are gathered in his name. May my life with you find a dwelling amid a community of friends. Help me to find partners and mentors who can encourage my faith, and to whom I can give as well. Lead me to those with whom I can join arms and find new strength to move forward. Amen.

14

Making Prayer in the Everyday

On one level, we may be thinking, discussing, seeing, calculating, meeting all the demands of external affairs. But deep within, behind the scenes, at a profounder level, we may also be in prayer and adoration, song and worship and a gentle receptiveness to divine breathings.

—THOMAS KELLY

The time of business does not with me differ from the time of prayer; and in the noise and clatter of my kitchen, while several persons are at the same time calling for different things, I possess God in as great tranquillity as if I were upon my knees at the blessed sacrament.

—BROTHER LAWRENCE

Once a friend who works with prison inmates invited me to come along. Getting into the prison compound was no easy matter. We had to pass through a tall fence topped with concertina coils of barbed wire. Once in the building, we stepped through a succession of steel-barred doors, each opened electronically by a barricaded guard.

When I first saw the inmates, they were filing into a cavernous dining hall for lunch. Surrounded by the prison's metal grays and dull olive-green walls, wearing standard-issue white uniforms, their line snaked down the corridor in wearying sameness.

But the several inmates gathered in the visitors' room were hungry for our company. According to prison policy, the visit had to be transacted across a wire-screened counter. Here we came as one of their few links with the outside world, and no direct contact was possible.

But I will never forget what happened toward the end of our time together. Two of the men agreed to sing a black gospel song, a cappella. Out of the cool barrenness of prison walls suddenly arose a smooth harmony and floating melody. The inmates' lonely monotony could not stop them from soulfully repeating the refrain "I went to church last night, and somethin' got a hold of me." It was breathtaking. I had not expected them to lead *me* into God's presence.

But I have been surprised again and again. I begin a day expecting the "same old same old," only to have my heart suddenly leap at the thought that God is already busy. Or five urgent projects "due yesterday" land on my desk and instead of panic I sense a steady, unflappable presence buoying me up. Or a wave of compassion for an acquaintance will well up from somewhere. The low grind of routine becomes infused with a beauty and power that I could not manufacture on my own. I even find myself humming under my breath, singing hymns of praise in very ordinary places.

I find that my everyday routine provides perfect opportunities to "practice the presence of God." It's tempting to think sometimes that I would be more spiritual living in a cabin, far from the harried and hurried pace of life. Many of us picture monks and nuns, sequestered from the pressures of what we call the real world. If we were to live like them, *then* we could focus on prayer, we think. And I do not doubt that some are called to a life of solitude. But I also know that most of us live in a world where colicky nine-month-olds keep parents awake through the night. It is here, in the stresses of earning a living and trying to get along with the in-laws, that most of us carry out our spiritual lives.

Everyday life is the only setting most of us have in which to grow in prayer. I find this entry from a few weeks ago in my journal: "Getting ready for an important meeting at work today, I spent time ironing a shirt and slacks. But I realized I could also *pray* about the day, the meeting, how God might want to use me, so that in those minutes I was preparing both physically and spiritually. As I would put on freshly starched and ironed clothes, so I would clothe myself in spiritual readiness." We can be praying underneath and through our activities, not just apart from them. We find that God's presence can be mediated through daily work, not destroyed by it. Christ himself was a carpenter most of his life; surely he sanctified those decades of labor with loving attention to God.

Kathryn Dillon, who works with Alzheimer's patients, practices what she calls a conscious-awareness prayer throughout the day: "When I am walking from room to room in the nursing home where I work and see someone and stop to interact, my internal voice is praying, 'Give me your love to show this person,' or 'Loan me your patience, Lord.' In the times when I am not interacting with anyone, but simply walking, I can go inside a bit and seek the active, living presence of God."

We do not need to wait until we're retired to get up early enough to read verses from the Bible. We do not have to go on month-long retreats to pause in the middle of a day for a few moments of prayer. For most of us, making more room for the spiritual life is not a matter of changing our daily lives, but reorienting our hearts. Growing in prayer is simply a matter of cultivating the garden plot we already have. "Walk and talk and work and laugh with your friends," wrote Quaker spiritual writer Thomas Kelly. "But behind the scenes, keep up the life of simple prayer and inward worship. Keep it up throughout the day. Let inward prayer be your last act before you fall asleep and the first act when you awake. And in time you will find, as did Brother Lawrence, that 'those who have the gale of the Holy Spirit go forward even in sleep.'"[1]

This can happen in some very simple ways. When activities and pressures lure me into forgetting, I find help in little devices. On my bathroom mirror, for example, I have taped an index card with the names of family members, friends, colleagues, and other people who need prayer. The card is so obvious that I see the name whenever I shave or brush my teeth, and I'm reminded to mention them in prayer. A friend of mine writes the name of someone she wants to pray for on a slip of paper and puts it in her coin purse. Each time she reaches in, she is reminded.

My mirror holds another reminder. A friend was praying for my writing of this book not long ago. One morning she felt the Lord gave her a distinct message: "Tell him it will go well. My hand is on this." She wrote it on a slip of paper. That little note, a divine communiqué to me during the long hours of writing, has continued to remind me that I am not alone, that all (thankfully!) does not hinge on my abilities.

I often turn downtimes into moments of prayer. I use some of my morning drive time to pray for the authors I work with daily, many of whom are writing books that will touch thousands of lives. Each morning as I enter my office, I make turning on my computer and desk lamp an occasion to remember that God is in control of my day. Or on my way home, when I cannot stop the day's events from swirling around inside, I not only relive the things I couldn't get done, the projects turned in on time (or not), the deals our company signed, I try also to gather all those thoughts and scenes into prayers. I carry my day into my praying.

And I carry my praying into my day. I try to take

prayerful walks. I savor a cup of tea and thank God for his goodness to me. When I jog in the morning, I take little cards with Scripture verses printed on them for meditation and memorizing. And I let music usher me into the presence of God—Bach, bluegrass, gospel. Historian of modern religion Martin Marty calls this hitchhiking, using the books and art forms and expressions of others to help us in devotion.[2]

If God is showing up in the ordinary turns and straight stretches of life, as I believe he is, it behooves us not to turn aside. We must allow God to stand our souls at attention wherever we are. To do that, we need to cultivate the ability to see and sense him.

Part of this for me means learning to be more present. I need to not be so submerged in my thoughts and schemes that I miss the signs of God's nearness. I am too often not "there" when he does act or speak. I am already *pre*occupied, packing full my time and space before I get there. That often keeps me also from experiencing God. But I want to be alert. I want to be open, not oblivious. People who have "abandoned themselves to God," as Jean-Pierre de Caussade wrote, "always lead mysterious lives and receive from him exceptional and miraculous gifts by means of the most ordinary, natural and chance experiences in which there appears to be nothing unusual. The simplest sermon, the most banal conversations, the least erudite books become a source of knowledge and wisdom to these souls by virtue of God's purpose.

This is why they carefully pick up the crumbs which clever minds tread under foot, for to them everything is precious and a source of enrichment."[3]

Once I was visiting William, my former neighbor. On the wall I saw a print of Vincent Van Gogh's famous painting of a vase with sunflowers. There was no mistaking the vivid palette and bold brushstrokes. William told me a story behind the painting. Some years before, William's doctor had told him he was suffering macular degeneration. He would slowly go blind. At the time when I visited him, his eyesight was indeed very dim. When he heard the terrible diagnosis, William immediately bought a ticket to Amsterdam. For a week he did nothing but make his way through the Van Gogh Museum, slowly soaking up the beauty and power of the paintings. He wanted to fill his mind with the images of a master. Never will I forget the story of a man who concentrated all his sight on what was beautiful and lasting.

There was something in the holy women and men of God through history that drove them to keep their eyes peeled. They stayed alert and attuned, even while going about active, fruitful lives. They conditioned their souls to recognize the holy and heavenly so that they did not miss it. Their lives were shot through with the presence of God, pervaded with the fragrance of grace. "Through some moment of beauty or pain," writes essayist and novelist Frederick Buechner, "some sudden turning of our lives, through some horror of the twelve o'clock news, some dream, . . . we catch a glimmer at least of what the saints are blinded by. Only then, unlike the saints, . . . we tend to go on as though nothing has happened. To go on as though something *has* happened is to enter that dimension of life that religion is a word for."[4] To go on is to *pray* and turn toward God.

You've heard the adage "Seeing is believing." Yet Jesus told someone that it is greater to believe even when you haven't seen (John 20:29). We get closed in sometimes, convinced that all that we see and experience now is the best we can hope for. We stop expecting much. We grind through one more task, dutifully showing up with an "I've been this way before" written across our faces.

Yet God has resources up his sleeve we know nothing of. He can do things we cannot even imagine. Expecting to meet a God of unlimited resources and creativity—believing it before we see it—prepares us to catch his surprising interventions.

Caroline McMillan advises early-childhood-education majors at a university in the Southeast. "One day," she recounts, "a new student came into my office."

He was huge and his mouth was sort of gaping open, which, combined with his weight, made him look incredibly dumb. I looked at his transcript—all D's and F's. As I despaired over where to start with this guy, it occurred to me that this might be a good time to pray. I thought to use my customary simple prayer, "Holy Lord, be with me now." I soon felt myself looking deeply into his eyes and *loving* this student. I realized I was in the presence of God—that God was in him, in me, in the room, and in our being together. I was filled with the most wonderful feeling of joy and serenity.

Life, more than we realize, is saturated with the miraculous. I know people who have been healed—dramatically, amazingly—when God chose to do so. I have heard story after story of medical conditions vanishing in response to prayer—too often to discount or explain them away.

But I also believe that many miracles escape our notice because we do not have eyes to see them. "Miracles," writes novelist Willa Cather in *Death Comes for the Archbishop*, "seem to me to rest not so much upon faces or voices or healing power coming suddenly near to us from afar off, but upon our perceptions being made finer, so that for a moment our eyes can see and our ears can hear what is there about us always."[5]

It's almost comical, the scene the biblical writer Luke paints in one of his stories. Jesus had just climbed a mountain to pray, when, as his disciples watched, "his face changed, and his clothes became as bright as a flash of lightning" (Luke 9:20). And the disciples *fell asleep*. Faced with the radiance of the splendor of God, they rubbed their eyes and stifled a few yawns. Ushered into the jolting presence of God, they curled up for a nap. But sleep here, as in other places in the Bible, represents more than a physical state. Sleepiness is a spiritual condition.

Too often I am plagued by a lack of wakefulness that

keeps me from seeing or hearing. A lack of alertness makes me miss the significance of small and great happenings. I sometimes enter prayer with a yawn that says, *I really don't expect much out of this.*

But, by the grace of God, there are other times. Times when I really smell the freshness of the earth outside my window after a rain. Times when my children wander into my study while I'm writing, and I notice them—really *see* them—for the first time in days. Times when I walk under a starlit sky and know that the One who displays his handiwork in the heavens brings his infinite creativity into my life as well.

We need to stay open to the eloquence and beauty and poignancy of God present in our lives. If we're willing, God will crack open our heavy-lidded eyes to see things we would surely otherwise miss. The God who never slumbers or sleeps (Psalm 121:4) will keep us from snoring our way through the wonder and adventure of living with him.

Once as I drove to work, I began to feel rising bitterness toward a colleague, someone I would work with that day. This person had snubbed me in the past, had been condescending, even nasty. My anger at her pettiness was already building. I was rehearsing in my mind how I could slight her in our meeting, be cool and distant in personal contact. But as I prayed, I began to see the possibility—even the summons—for another way. I could be bigger than all this. I saw as I prayed that a person with God's intentions at heart would overcome unpleasantness with good, not with more bitterness.

And what a difference that made! I was cordial from the moment I bumped into her as we met in the parking lot. And she, too, this time was warm. I felt reconciliation taking place. A mundane, ordinary day was transfigured. Prayer had injected a new element into a day-in, day-out relationship. God made a difference.

If "the heavens are telling the glory of God," as the psalmist sang, God save us from slumber. There is too much to see, to notice, to know, for us to spend our lives sleepy or unaware. Whether through a spine-tingling healing or through more quiet evidence of the slow work of God, prayer can condition us to be more awake. We will find that God's presence makes life very eloquent.

Prayers

Teach me, my God and King,
In all things thee to see,
and what I do in anything
To do it as for thee.
—GEORGE HERBERT (SEVENTEENTH CENTURY)[6]

Forth in your name, O Lord, I go,
My daily labor to pursue,
You, only you, resolved to know
In all I think, or speak or do.
—CHARLES WESLEY (EIGHTEENTH CENTURY)[7]

15

Letting Go and Being Led

Whenever you pray, you profess that you are not
God and that you wouldn't want to be, that you
haven't reached your goal yet, and that you never will
reach it in this life, that you must constantly stretch
out your hands and wait again for the gift which gives
new life.

—HENRI NOUWEN

While he strips of everything the souls who give themselves absolutely to him, God gives them something which
takes the place of all: his love.

—JEAN-PIERRE DE CAUSSADE

"It has been a struggle," begins an entry in my journal almost ten years ago. "I worry endlessly about job opportunities, the move to Indiana, selling our house. But most of all I wrestle with my career."

A lot was happening in my life. As I prayed, talked with others, and daydreamed. I had begun to sense a shift in my vocation: a call to writing and editing. I was honestly perplexed. I had had no journalism training in college. I had done some freelance writing, but not enough to launch a career. And at thirty-one I could hardly think about returning to college; I had to provide for a family and owned a house I couldn't seem to sell.

But my worries turned into prayers as my journal entry continued: "All I can do, Lord, is wait and allow you to fit all the pieces together. Help me to know that you are working everything out according to your will. Use today to allow me to believe again in your goodness." In the entries for the days and months that followed, I often came to God with my hands clenched with worry, only to feel them gently opening. In prayer I was able to let go, to give up my worries and anxieties to God.

It may be only after long struggle, but I have found the prayer of relinquishment, as some call it, to be an essential part of the spiritual life. It could seem, on the surface, like a dreary activity. The language of giving up does not come easily to our lips. And sometimes it *is* an exercise in sheer trust to submit to God. But I have consistently found that surrender and self-abandonment lead to moments of great spiritual progress.

―――――

Relinquishment begins with acknowledging that much of life lies beyond our control. We set our goals and make our plans, but who can be sure? Who can guarantee that our projects and programs will work tomorrow, or that we will even have tomorrow? Of course, much of the time we would prefer to organize and orchestrate. We are drawn to magazine articles with titles like "How to Get What You Want and Protect What You Have." But when we maintain our plans and feel in control of our future, we lull ourselves into forgetting that we cannot make the sun rise.

Tragedy can wake us up to the reality of our lack of control. Suffering causes a kind of upheaval in our routine. It leaves us with pain we did not want and loss we would do anything to avoid. We may rebel, we may rage, but we cannot undo what happened. And at such times we see, perhaps more clearly than at any other time, our powerlessness. To be sure, we are called to do many things—vigorously—in life; passivity is no virtue. But letting go is in a real sense acknowledging what *is*: We are only a small part of a whole. Our plans are not everything. We admit that even our routine is vulnerable to forces beyond our control.

Many people hit this truth hard at midlife. "I woke up one morning," writes one executive, "and realized I was never going to make a million dollars, my marriage was never going to meet my wildest expectations, my children were grown and didn't need me anymore—and this was going to be all there was."[1] We see that not all our ambitions are reachable. Our talents are finite. Opportunities do not come in endless supply. Such moments jar us awake to the fact that we cannot "have it all," that we cannot go on with life as always and never give an inch.

"Unless a kernel of wheat falls to the ground and dies," said Jesus in John 12:24–25, "it remains only a single seed. But if it dies, it produces many seeds. The man who loves his life will lose it, while the man who hates his life in the world will keep it for eternal life." Only by "dying to" the life that we know, says Jesus, do we find real life. And relinquishment is a kind of dying: to our illusion of self-mastery, to our insistence that we always "do it my way." Perhaps that is what Søren Kierkegaard meant when he said that "God creates everything out of nothing—and everything that God is to use he first reduces to nothing."[2] We need a certain humility and vulnerability for God to use us.

At such times we find ourselves ready to go beyond "my will be done" to "your will be done." We pray that God will make us open to the ways he wants to shape and mold us. We picture ourselves not as a finished vase but as clay in the potter's hands. This may be a dramatic enough shift that it feels like conversion, a radical reorientation of our minds, hearts, wills, and souls. We "turn the face of our inner self entirely in His direction," in Thomas Merton's memorable words, perhaps for the first time.[3]

As we pray prayers of relinquishment, we will discover how much our lives are full of specific wants and wishes. We set our hearts on a job opening. We hope for a higher salary. We want our children to choose to go to college. We ask for healing.

These and many other wants tumble out in our petitions. And that is as it should be. If our desires belong anywhere, it is in prayer. But we can voice our wants in more than one way. We can pray by insisting on a certain thing, concluding that only if God gives us what we want will we find security. But we thereby lose sight of other options, that there can even *be* other options.

There is another way. While we say, "Lord, this is what I want," we also do not get too tied to the final answer. We face into God not with just desire but with open-ended trust. Not only with longing but also with hope. Contemplative writer Macrina Wiederkehr makes an interesting distinction along these lines. Rather than pray *for* the things she needs, she has begun to pray *about* them. "When I pray *for* something," she writes, "my prayer tends to be much more narrow. I put expectations on God. I expect something definite to happen and I am disappointed if it doesn't happen. . . . But when I pray *about* something I am putting expectations on myself. I focus on the presence of God in my specific problem and we look at it together, God and I."[4] We want what we ask for, of course; we pray with faith, believing, but we acknowledge that the One who hears will do good no matter what transpires. Our prayer is directed not so much to the gift as to the Giver.

Until recently my friend Jan Senn worked as a magazine editor in a Chicago suburb. A harassing neighbor at her apartment building drove her to live in a motel for several weeks while she searched for another place she could afford. "But I kept running up against closed doors," she wrote me. "So I finally realized that instead of presenting God with three options I could live with, I needed to ask God what *he* wanted me to do. I got to the point where I was able to say to God, 'whatever.' " That became her prayer of relinquishment.

It also became the turning point. Through a series of events she sees as providential, she was offered a position at a spiritual retreat house in another state, a job that combines her skills and background in ways that still leave her amazed. She did not get what she first wanted, of course: No apartment turned up. But she met the Answerer. And he gave her something else. Something even better.

Prayers of relinquishment are powerful because they give God berth. They give him space in which to move and act. They do not obliterate our wills, but transform them. They serve as a kind of invitation for his power and presence.

"What God most longs to discover in us," writes Macrina Wiederkehr, "is our willingness to embrace ourselves as we were at our beginning—empty, little, and poor. Our willingness gives God free space within us to work out the Divine Plan. Our potential for greatness is tremendous. Acceptance of our littleness makes it possible for our greatness to emerge. Our littleness is not a choice. It is simply the way we are. Our greatness, however, is a choice. When we choose to accept the life God has given to us, when we allow God to fill our emptiness, we are choosing greatness."[5]

We see this in Paul the apostle. He struggled with God, three times pleading that God remove a "thorn in the flesh"—some illness or chronic condition. The Lord came back each time with only the promise that "My grace is sufficient for you, for my power is made perfect in weakness" (2 Corinthians 12:8). Paul ends up "delighting" in his weaknesses because in them God's power had room to work. And what a power it was! Paul, a man who sometimes addressed his first-century crowds with "weakness and fear, and much trembling," was perhaps more responsible for the spread of Christianity worldwide than anyone. Paul never was healed, but God worked through Paul with astonishing power. His relinquishment became a time not of defeat but of opening to One who has ultimate power over any obstacle. An ability beyond human reckoning was released. So in losing our lives, we find them (Mark 8:35). By giving up we gain far more than we would ever possess on our own.

It is not hard to see, then, that relinquishment is not the same as resignation. We are not talking about a droopy, I-couldn't-care-less-what-happens outlook. "Resignation," as writer Catherine Marshall notes, "lies down in the dust of a godless universe and steels itself for the worst."[6] Relinquishment, on the other hand, says, "I choose to believe that God has a solution for it." One grows out of depression and lack of belief. The other takes the moment at hand and marries it to hope.

Think of a garden scene in what is perhaps Western history's best-known example of relinquishment: Jesus on the night before his death by crucifixion. We see him in the Garden of Gethsemane saying, "Take this cup from me. Yet not what I will, but what you will." But *before* that poignant acceptance of God's purposes, he says, "*Abba*, Father, everything is possible for you" (Mark 14:35–36). It was his conviction that God was *Abba*, sometimes translated as "Daddy," that allowed him to merge his purposes into God's. It was not sheer determination but a conviction that a caring, father-like God held all possibilities in his hands. If the worst happened, even then God would work good. His Crucifixion would have a Resurrection attached to it.

I am told that our English phrase *self-surrender*, which has overtones of defeat and grudging submission, finds a different sense in the French equivalent. *Se livrer* means "to hand over or deliver oneself to in a freely chosen act of love." To surrender in this meaning "is a total turning to God in self-giving, a response to a gesture of love."[7]

Relinquishment, then, is not leaping into some vast cosmic unknown. It is becoming willing to be led by a Good Shepherd. It is to hold lightly our lives, which were first given by a God of love. When we pray "your kingdom come," we are not stumbling along with a God of chance or caprice. We are submitting to a God who has plans of good for us, not evil. "God's gifts put man's best dreams to shame," wrote poet Elizabeth Barrett Browning. He has resources and plans that would boggle our imaginations.

Yes, it feels risky sometimes. But why let our fear of what we cannot see keep us from giving ourselves to the One who sees all?

Some years ago, to pastor Dale Galloway's great grief, his wife asked for a divorce. "Many times as a minister," he wrote, "I have heard people talk like they thought there were some things worse than death. At that moment and in the following days for me, life was worse than death." But then in his desolation he offered a prayer of relinquishment:

> I practiced what I call "let go and let God." I took my hands and cupped them in front of me, held them up, and verbally put inside those hands everything I was fretting over and didn't have any answers to. I said out loud as I held up both hands, "There it is, God; I can't change it, I don't know what to do with it, it's all so unacceptable to me. I have been fighting it. I just don't know what to do. There it is, Lord, I give it all to you. I give to you what people think about me." As I talked to God, I turned my hands upside down and said, "There it is, Lord. It's all yours." As I stretched my fingers out as far as I could, turning my hands upside down so that it was impossible to hold on to anything, as I dropped my arms to

my side, a wonderful feeling of serenity suddenly spread throughout my entire being. I now had peace in the midst of the storm.[8]

Our prayers of release and acceptance need not be elaborate. We need not worry much about the words. More than anything, a prayer of letting go is coming into God's presence with our agendas quieted. It is reverently opening our life and heart to a God of infinite possibilities.

This morning as I prayed—thinking about the day ahead of writing, family responsibilities, house chores—I prayed, "I give you my life, Lord. Please take it and use me." There were no crashing cymbals in the air above me. I felt no jolts of spiritual electricity. But what I said had huge import. I opened myself to a great Love and Power. In a kind of self-emptying, I made myself available to be filled.

Many times as I pray such prayers, I find it helpful to gently hold my hands open, palms upward. The customary prayer posture in the first decades of the church's life, scholars tell us, was different from what we have learned during childhood table graces: not hunched over, hands clasped together. Prayer was a bodily attitude of open hands and outstretched arms.

I like that window on openness. It helps in praying to unclasp my hands and release my heart to the surprises God wants to work. I expect God to reveal more and use me more as my grip loosens and my control relaxes.

My relinquishment is not always perfect, of course.

Sometimes my surrender of self is partial. And many times during each day I mentally take back my life to make things turn out as I want. But God can use even our imperfect offerings of self. He has gotten used to my occasional reservations and protests. Intention is what matters, not perfection. God, from whom all that is good comes, will take my simple offering and carry forward his plans and purposes.

And I am trying to discover the art of relinquishing each part of my day. As I walk through the scenes of my busy, filled schedule, I can hand it all back to God. I can consciously make room for the One who can make all the difference. It can be as simple as a murmured "I have faith in you, Lord." Saying such prayers can help us get ourselves out of the way and give God room to move.

On the morning I penned the journal entry that began this chapter, I could never have foreseen what would happen. Within months I was offered a half-time job—writing a college centennial history. I found a part-time position at a church in our new location. I had no trouble getting freelance writing assignments. And when the college history book was done, a national magazine offered me a full-time job as an editor. The opportunities that opened up far exceeded what I could ever have made happen myself.

I know relinquishing prayer will not always be easy.

I will no doubt cling to new schemes and prospects that at the time seem too good to let go of. But I am learning that by releasing I receive. In letting go I am held safe. So I trust God to help me find the courage to release my grip.

Prayers

Father, for such a long time I have pleaded before You this, the deep desire of my heart:_____. Yet the more I've clamored for Your help with this, the more remote You have seemed.

I confess my demanding spirit in this matter. I've tried suggesting to You ways my prayer could be answered. To my shame, I've even bargained with You. Yet I know that trying to manipulate the Lord of the Universe is utter foolishness. No wonder my spirit is so sore and weary!

I want to trust you, Father. My spirit knows that these verities are forever trustworthy even when I feel nothing. . . .

That You are there.
    (You said, "Lo, I am with you always.")
That You love me.
    (You said, "I have loved thee with an everlasting love.")
That You alone know what is best for me.
    (For in You, Lord, "are hid all the treasures of wisdom and knowledge.")

Perhaps all along, You have been waiting for me to give up all self-effort. At last I want You in my life even more than I want _____ . So now, by an act of my will I relinquish this to You. I will accept Your will, whatever that may be. Thank You for counting this act of my will as the decision of the real person even when my emotions protest. I ask You to hold me true to this decision. To You, Lord God, who alone are worthy, I bend the knee with thanksgiving that this too will "work together for the good." Amen.

—CATHERINE MARSHALL[9]

16

Moving Forward

Our pursuit of God is successful just because he is forever seeking to manifest himself to us.

—A. W. TOZER

The Living Christ within us is the initiator and we are the responders. God the Lover, the accuser, the revealer of light and darkness presses within us. "Behold I stand at the door and knock." And all our apparent initiative is already a response.

—THOMAS KELLY

Because I missed making it to my father's hospital bedside before he died, he and I never got a chance to do some important talking. I had things to say, emotional closure I wanted to bring. And there were questions to ask: I knew very little about his financial affairs, and nothing about provisions he had made for Mother.

Later that evening, back at my parents' Santa Monica home, I began going through Dad's papers and records. I didn't know what to expect. Fortunately most of the bills and canceled checks and passbooks were in one place—a hallway closet next to my old bedroom, which Dad had turned into his home office. To my surprise, I also found a copy of the family will, which I had never seen and had heard him mention only in passing. I trembled inwardly as I opened it. There had been a few years of strain in our relationship, even a time when I was shunned for marrying against his and Mom's wishes. Would I be mentioned? It was not the money I cared about, but my standing in the family.

But there was my name—even my children's! He had decreed to me a full share of the inheritance. I grieved his passing, sorrowed not to have bid a final farewell, but at least I knew my status. There was no lingering question about how he saw me.

We have similar fears, perhaps not always rational, about our relationship with God. Can we always count on his loving us and walking with us? When we rail at him or feel his absence, can we keep going in trust?

With questions like these in the background, I want to explore how prayer grows in the deep places of our hearts. And how does it become an ongoing part of our lives? To do so, it helps me to think of progress in prayer in terms of three metaphors: gift, journey, and adventure.

Growth in Prayer Is a Gift

Often in this book I have looked at *how* prayer is done. I have tried to be intensely practical about what we do. But much of what happens when we pray comes from outside of us, from God's side of the equation. This is not to say we become passive, only that we should not feel that it all depends on us. Spirituality is not a decathlon where sheer grit and buckets of perspiration determine the final outcome. Nor is it tied to some private religious "talent" or spiritual genius.

A relationship with God is something we receive, not achieve. It is not a reward but a present. It is not something we earn but something we are given. And just as salvation begins with letting go of the accomplishments we think make us presentable to God, so does our growth in the Spirit. We come not pushing but letting ourselves be pulled.

Prayer has mostly to do with God. His grace. His willingness. His invitation. What we say in our devotional times is our response to God's invitation. Prayer is not some bright idea *we've* thought of. In Jesus Christ, God opened the door. In prayer we walk through.

Once a radio talk-show host interviewed me on angels. I will never forget the plaintive remarks of one call-in listener. She confessed to having difficulty in praying. "But what I do," she said, "is just give my prayers to my angels, and let them carry my requests up to God." She reasoned that God must be aloof and inaccessible. But that is not the case. Because God himself invites us to pray, because he does not reside in a far-off heavenly realm, we do not need to turn to celestial stand-ins or reconcile ourselves to a distant deity. God is actually eager to hear our prayers.

Some religious traditions say we pray to get through to God. Making connection with the Absolute is *our* job, and sometimes a difficult one at that. But the wisest spiritual traditions stress that the point is not that we find God but that he has found us. We don't pray to reach out as much as to reply. Salvation, the Bible's word for our rescue from our prisons of self and sin, is not our doing but God's. We accept what God has done. That is what the coming of Jesus means. That is the good news of Christianity. That is the good news about prayer.

Vincent Donovan lived for a time in Tanzania, teaching and preaching among the Masai people. One day he was talking with a Masai elder about the struggles of believing in God. The elder was pointing out that the Masai word Vincent had used to translate the word *faith* was not very satisfactory. That word meant only "to agree to."

He said to believe like that was similar to a white hunter shooting an animal with his gun from a great distance. Only his eyes and his fingers took part in the act. We should find another word. He said for a man really to believe is like a lion going after its prey. . . . His legs give him the speed to catch it. All the power of his body is involved in the terrible death leap and single blow to the neck with the front paw, the blow that actually kills. And as the animal goes down the lion envelops it in his arms, . . . pulls it to himself, and makes it part of himself. This is the way a lion kills. This is the way a man believes. . . .

But my wise old teacher was not finished yet.

"We did not search you out, Padri," he said to me. "We did not even want you to come to us. . . . You followed us away from your house into the bush, into the plains, into the steppes where our cattle are, . . . into our villages, into our homes. You told us of the High God, how we must search for him, . . . We have not left our land. We have not searched for him. . . . He has searched *us* out and found us. All the time we think we are the lion. In the end, the lion is God."[1]

For centuries Christian theologians have debated the meaning of Jesus' death on the cross. Their "theories of the Atonement" certainly shed light on this focal point in many believers' devotion. But consider this bare-bones summary: The cross means that intimacy with God is wildly, wonderfully possible. The guilt and shame and frustration that sometimes make prayer seem out of reach need not make us halt or hover. God will not allow a breakdown in fellowship with him to be the last word. He comes among us in his own Son to restore what has been broken and devastated. Finally we are freed from the burden of living moral, spiritual lives in order to be saved. We experience Christ's salvation power so that we *can* live the lives God intends. We simply ask God to make it so. We ask him to make what Christ did real for our lives.

"He bore with us," wrote an anonymous third-century writer, "and in pity [God] took upon himself and gave his own Son as a ransom for us—the Holy for the wicked, the Sinless for sinners, the Just for the unjust, the Incorrupt for the corrupt, the Immortal for the mortal. . . . O sweet exchange! . . . O benefits unhoped for!"[2]

This giftlike quality is not just for our beginnings. We stay open to the way God "gifts" our praying throughout all of life, knowing that beyond our efforts will always be possibilities we could never have dreamed of. We come expectantly. Which means the spiritual life will sometimes surprise us. We may trudge through months—years?—where little seems to happen. Other times we will find ourselves intoxicated by God. The Bible, after all, paints pictures of wilderness fasts and forty-day temptations with one stroke and of being drunk with the Holy Spirit with the next.

I have already talked about the dry times. So here I want to talk about the times when prayer "takes off." Here, for example, is a quiet Quaker scholar, Thomas Kelly, who decades ago penned a spiritual classic called *A Testament of Devotion*:

There come times when prayer pours forth in volumes and originality such as we cannot create. It rolls through us like a mighty tide. Our prayers are mingled with a vaster Word, a Word that at one time was made flesh. We pray, and yet it is not we who pray, but a Greater who prays in us. Something of our punctiform selfhood is weakened, but never lost. All we can say is, Prayer is taking place, and I am given to be in the orbit.[3]

Or here is John Cassian, a monk from centuries ago, describing what he calls the "prayer of fire":

that ineffable prayer which rises above human consciousness, with no voice sounding, no tongue moving, no words uttered. The soul lights up with heavenly illumination and no longer employs constricted, human speech. All sensibility is gathered together and, as though from some very abundant source, the soul breaks forth richly, bursts out unspeakably to God, and in the tiniest instant it pours out so much more than the soul can either describe or remember when it returns to itself.[4]

We cannot force such moments. But we can wait. We can prepare the ground. And then every now and then, very often when we least expect it, God will give our prayers flight. What had been a discipline becomes an art. Our stumbling words are lifted into song. We "pray in the Spirit," to use Paul the apostle's phrase, lofted above the normal constraints.

"I play in a symphony orchestra," one Internet friend of mine writes. "There are times when the entire group of eighty musicians becomes inspired—we don't know why—and we play absolutely magnificently. We all say, 'What happened?' No one can answer. It happens in the spiritual life also."

It happens in my praying sometimes. My heart pours forth its longings without faltering. Or I feel an overflowing love for God that needs no scripting. My normal speech seems so limited that I pray in unknown tongues, the sounds and syllables streaming out in effortless stirring.

I can only call those moments gifts, foretastes of the communion we will enjoy in heaven.

Growth in Prayer Is a Journey

One of the biblical tradition's rich images for life with God is that of a path or road. We follow a way. People who pray are more like pilgrims than they are settlers. There is always something more God leads us to. We pitch a tent every now and then, but we do not settle for good. People who pray are more like pioneers than they are settlers.

Do we never stop on this path? Are we always seeking God? In one sense our search is over; for in our seeking we have been found. God has met us and made us his own. The Bible uses the wonderful, reassuring language of family: We are children of a loving Father. Whether the image is of having been born anew or of having been adopted, we have an irrevocable place in God's family. No wall or abyss jeopardizes that communion.

But in another sense the searching and seeking never end.

Here the Bible shifts metaphors, from parent and child to husband and wife: God is "married" to his people. Christ is a bridegroom, his church the bride. The kingdom of God is a marriage supper. If a human marriage relationship can deepen and become richer through a lifetime, how much more a relationship with a God of inexhaustible love! The first taste of intimacy, the first discovery of God's wondrous presence, is followed by another. And another. And on it goes. To find that we can talk to God is the mere starting point. We are lured on to experience more and more of the ineffable joys of being filled with God. That search for greater intimacy is never finished, and it grows more thrilling the farther one proceeds.

I remember once mentioning spiritual restlessness in a positive way to a friend. He was taken aback. He thought that since he had committed his life to God, his restlessness would forever cease. For him a restless heart meant agitated bewilderment. I tried to help him reclaim the holy value of restlessness. Because we are touched by God's love, I might have told him, we will always long for his embrace. When we see the Beautiful, we are never satisfied with a glimpse. When we taste God's sweetness, we will find our spiritual hunger deepening. We will want more, and that will lead us forward. "You called and cried out loud," wrote Augustine, "and shattered my deafness. You were radiant and resplendent, you put to flight my blindness. You were fragrant, and I drew in my breath and now pant after you. I tasted you, and I feel but hunger and thirst for you. You touched me, and I am set on fire to attain the peace which is yours."[5]

Growth in Prayer Is an Adventure

Life with God is beyond my predicting or imagining. It can never be reduced to the tidy or known. The dictionary definition of the word *adventure* spells out what we know intuitively about prayer: It is "a bold and usually risky undertaking."

I read recently about a book with an intriguing title: *The Courage to Pray*. I have prayed about having courage, but courage *to pray?* The more I think about it, the more sense it makes. What if the untamable God we approach (and assume we know) turns our conceptions upside down? If prayer puts us in relationship with God, who can guarantee that we won't be changed by the encounter? So something in us wants to hold back from intimacy with God, from all the unpredictability of its potential power. "I've been praying for you," my friend Steve Brown once wrote me. "But if things get too bad, let me know, and I'll let up." Praying is not the safest activity in the world. To say God will not leave us alone contains two meanings: Not only will he not leave us stranded, he will not leave us the same. When we follow, we can expect him to lead us to places we would never have gone on our own.

We can also expect times when we do not know what is next. One day some years ago I set out on my regular jogging route. Because of the dense morning fog I could barely make out turns in the path ahead. Only by recognizing wayside bushes and fences and other markers could I keep my feet on the trail that finally led home. In my life with God I usually see only a few curves and turns in front of me. I follow One whose ways are beyond imagining. Who can say where God will take me?

> Oh, the depth of the riches of the
>   wisdom and knowledge of God!
> How unsearchable his judgments,
>   and his paths beyond tracing out! (Romans 11:33)

Which is why another definition of *adventure* also fits: "an exciting undertaking." Precisely because God is beyond our predicting, prayer will not be boring. As in the title of a book by a friend, prayer is *Living by God's Surprises*.[6] We think we want to be in control. But in our deeper selves we want something more than predictability. We want Someone larger than ourselves to lift our lives out of the ordinary. In the first book of C. S. Lewis's fanciful *Chronicles of Narnia*, Mr. Beaver tries to describe to the children Aslan, the lion, the Christ-figure, who is wild and free and comes at will:

> "I tell you he is the King of the wood and the son of
> the great Emperor-Beyond-the-Sea. Don't you know

who is the King of Beasts? Aslan is a lion—*the* Lion, the great Lion."

"Ooh!" said Susan. "I'd thought he was a man. Is he—quite safe? I shall feel rather nervous about meeting a lion."

"That you will, dearie, and no mistake," said Mrs. Beaver, "if there's anyone who can appear before Aslan without their knees knocking, they're either braver than most or else just silly."

"Then he isn't safe?"

"Safe?" said Mr. Beaver. "Don't you hear what Mrs. Beaver tells you? Who said anything about safe? 'Course he isn't safe. But he's good. He's the King, I tell you."

"I'm longing to see him," said Peter, "even if I do feel frightened when it comes to the point."[7]

God is the awe-inspiring, frightening, but gracious King who leads us into adventure.

So I keep praying. Some mornings I manage little better than a groggy, distracted few minutes. Other times I'm moved to tears; mere technique becomes art. One week I may not feel much of anything. Then one day a glimpse of God's fiery power leaves me quietly elated for hours. The constant is God. And usually, when I sense him, I cannot help wanting to be with him. And sensing that he stands listening, I cannot help talking to him.

Prayer

Lord, your Word says,
"No eye has seen,
no ear has heard,
no mind has conceived
what God has prepared for those who love him."

Help me in all my days to at least glimpse the wonders of your goodness and mercy. Amen.

Afterword

I am interested in hearing about ways this book helped you in your praying. And I am interested in hearing how you experience God in daily life. Please write to me at P.O. Box 968, Nolensville, Tennessee 37135.

Notes

Introduction: The First Steps

1. Kenneth Woodward, "Talking to God," *Newsweek*, January 6, 1992, p. 39.

2. Saint Augustine, *Confessions*, trans. Henry Chadwick (Oxford, Eng.: Oxford University Press, 1991), p. 3.

3. Anna Quindlen, *One True Thing* (New York: Random House, 1994), p. 59.

4. John Powell, *He Touched Me* (Niles, Ill.: Argus Communications, 1974), p. 50.

5. Larry Dossey, *Healing Words* (San Francisco: HarperSanFrancisco, 1993).

6. Henri Nouwen, *Life of the Beloved* (New York: Crossroad, 1992), pp. 37–38.

7. Saint Augustine, *Confessions*, p. 3.

8. Søren Kierkegaard, quoted in *The Lion Prayer Collection*, ed. Mary Batchelor (Oxford, Eng.: Lion, 1992), p. 13.

1: A Cry for Help

1. Dom Chapman, quoted in Richard Foster, *Prayer: Finding the Heart's True Home* (San Francisco: HarperSanFrancisco, 1992), p. 7.

2. Brother Giles, "The Sayings of Brother Giles," *The Little Flowers of St. Francis*, trans. Raphael Brown (New York: Doubleday, 1958), p. 278.

3. Quoted in Edythe Draper, *Draper's Book of Quotations for the Christian World* (Wheaton, Ill.: Tyndale House, 1992), p. 480.

4. Ecclesiastes 5:2b.

5. Joan Wester Anderson, *Where Miracles Happen* (New York: Ballantine Books, 1994), pp. 32–33.

6. Michael Allen, *This Time This Place* (Indianapolis: Bobbs-Merrill, 1971), p. 117.

7. Ann and Barry Ulanov, *Primary Speech* (Atlanta: John Knox, 1982), p. 15.

8. Adapted from Augustine, *Soliloquies*, quoted in *The Macmillan Book of Earliest Christian Prayers*, ed. F. Forrester Church and Terrence J. Mulry. (New York: Collier/Macmillan, 1988), pp. 236–37.

2: The Simplest Language in the World

1. Quoted in *The Beginning of Wisdom*, ed. Thomas Becknell and Mary Ellen Ashcroft (Nashville: Moorings, 1995), p. 3.

2. Sandra Goodwin Clopine, quoted in Jim Castelli, *How I Pray* (New York: Ballantine Books, 1994), p. 21.

3. Gerald May, *The Awakened Heart* (San Francisco: HarperSanFrancisco, 1991), p. 60.

4. Quoted in Henri Nouwen, *The Way of the Heart* (New York: Ballantine Books, 1981), p. 64.

5. Thérèse of Lisieux, *Autobiography of St. Thérèse of Lisieux*, trans. Ronald Knox (New York: P. J. Kenedy, 1958), quoted in *Spiritual Power*, ed. Sherwood Eliot Wirt (Westchester, Ill.: Crossway, 1989), p. 105.

6. *Midrash Tehillim* 5.6, quoted in James H. Charlesworth, "Jewish Prayers in the Time of Jesus," *The Princeton Seminary Bulletin*, supplementary issue no. 2 (1992): 47.

7. Ibid., p. 48.

3: A Quietness of Soul

1. Richard Foster, *Prayer* (San Francisco: HarperSanFrancisco, 1992), p. 1.

2. Quoted in Nicholas Dawidoff, "Only the Typewriter Is Silent," *The New York Times*, August 10, 1995.

3. Quoted in Edythe Draper, *Draper's Book of Quotations for the Christian World* (Wheaton, Ill.: Tyndale House, 1992), p. 563.

4. Cornelius Plantinga, Jr., "Background Noise," *Christianity Today*, July 17, 1995, p. 42.

5. Quoted in Robert Llewelyn, Kallistos Ware, and Mary Clare, *Praying Home* (Cambridge, Mass.: Cowley, 1987), p. 43.

6. Quoted in Henri Nouwen, *The Way of the Heart* (New York: Ballantine Books, 1981), pp. 37–38.

7. Susan Annette Muto, *Pathways of Spiritual Living*, quoted in Bob Benson, Sr., and Michael W. Benson, *Disciplines for the Inner Life* (Nashville: Thomas Nelson Publishers, 1989), p. 76.

8. Cornelius Plantinga, Jr., "Background Noise," p. 42.

9. Henri Nouwen, *The Way of the Heart* (New York: Ballantine Books, 1981), p. 65.

10. Iris Cully, *Education for Spiritual Growth* (San Francisco: Harper & Row, 1978), p. 54.

11. Quoted in George Gallup, Jr., and Timothy Jones, *The Saints Among Us* (Harrisburg, Pa.: Morehouse, 1992), p. 55.

4: *The Way of Intimacy*

1. Quoted in Ramona Cramer Tucker, "Susan Ashton, Home at Last," *Today's Christian Woman*, November–December 1995, p. 47.

2. Morton Hunt, *The Universe Within* (New York: Simon and Schuster, 1982), pp. 222–23.

3. Simone Weil, *Waiting for God* (New York: Harper Colophon/Harper & Row, 1951), pp. 68–69.

4. Ibid.

5. Robert Coles, *The Spiritual Life of Children* (Boston: Houghton Mifflin, 1990), p. 40.

6. Bilquis Sheikh, *I Dared to Call Him Father* (Eastbourne, Eng.: Kingsway, 1979), pp. 51–53, quoted in Roger Pooley and Philip Seddon, *The Lord of the Journey* (London: Collins, 1986), pp. 90–91.

7. Reynolds Price, "The Gospel According to Saint John," *Incarnation* (New York: Penguin Books, 1990), p. 72.

5: Facing Our Failings: When We Know We've Blown It

1. Harry Crews, quoted in *Modern American Memoirs*, ed. Annie Dillard and Cort Conley (New York: HarperCollins, 1995), pp. 8–9.

2. Charles Colson, *Born Again* (Grand Rapids, Mich.: Fleming H. Revell, 1976, 1977, 1995), pp. 113, 116–117.

3. William Shakespeare, *King Lear*, in *Four Tragedies*, ed. David Bevington (New York: Bantam Books, 1980), pp. 434–35.

4. Kenneth Woodward, "Do We Need Satan?" *Newsweek*, November 13, 1995, pp. 63–64.

5. Isaac the Syrian, quoted in Alan E. Nelson, *Broken in the Right Place* (Nashville: Thomas Nelson, 1993), p. 88.

6. Martin Luther, quoted in *The Lord of the Journey*, ed. Roger Pooley and Philip Seddon (London: Collins, 1986), p. 124.

7. John Morison, quoted in *The Lion Prayer Collection*, ed. Mary Batchelor (Oxford, Eng.: Lion, 1992), p. 47.

6: Celebrating God

1. Gale D. Webbe, "The Toughest Virtue," *Christianity Today*, November 9, 1984, p. 82.

2. Richard L. Pratt, *Pray with Your Eyes Open* (Phillipsburg, N.J.: Presbyterian and Reformed, 1988), p. 27.

3. C. S. Lewis, *Letters to Malcolm: Chiefly on Prayer* (New York: Harcourt Brace Jovanovich, 1963), p. 90.

4. C. S. Lewis, *Reflections on the Psalms* (New York: Harcourt, Brace, 1958), pp. 90–91.

5. Brother Lawrence, *The Practice of the Presence of God* (New York: Doubleday, 1977), p. 68.

6. Mary Batchelor, ed., *The Lion Prayer Collection* (Oxford, Eng.: Lion, 1992), p. 36.

7: Not Being Afraid to Ask

1. C. S. Lewis, *Letters to Malcolm: Chiefly on Prayer* (New York: Harcourt Brace Jovanovich, 1963), pp. 19–20.

2. Rosemary Ellen Guiley, *The Miracle of Prayer* (New York: Pocket Books, 1995), p. 217.

3. I am indebted to C. S. Lewis for this image, which, in slightly different form, appeared in *Letters to Malcolm*, pp. 55–56.

4. Quoted in Madeleine L'Engle, *Two-Part Invention* (New York: Harper & Row, 1988), pp. 185–86.

5. Anselm, quoted in *The Lion Prayer Collection*, ed. Mary Batchelor (Oxford, Eng.: Lion, 1992), p. 234.

8: Getting Real with God: Emotions in Prayer

1. Thomas Merton, *Thoughts in Solitude* (Boston: Shambhala, 1956), p. 14.

2. Elie Wiesel, *All Rivers Run to the Sea* (New York: Alfred A. Knopf, 1995), p. 84.

3. Richard Foster, *Prayer* (San Francisco: HarperSanFrancisco, 1992), p. 23.

4. Frank Bianco, *Voices of Silence* (New York: Anchor Books/Doubleday, 1991), pp. xi–xx, passim. (Originally published by Paragon House.)

9: Listening for God in Our Lives

1. Lily Tomlin, quoted in Dallas Willard, *In Search of Guidance* (San Francisco: HarperSanFrancisco/Grand Rapids, Mich.: Zondervan, 1993), p. 6.

2. Madeleine L'Engle, *Two-Part Invention* (New York: Harper & Row, 1988), pp. 123–24.

3. C. S. Lewis, *The Problem of Pain* (New York: Macmillan, 1947), p. 81.

4. Quoted in Carin Rubenstein, "Your Spiritual Self," *New Woman*, March 1995, pp. 86–87.

5. Quoted in Philip Yancey, *Finding God in Unexpected Places* (Nashville: Moorings, 1994), p. 210.

6. Frank Colquhoun, quoted in *The Lion Prayer Collection*, ed. Mary Batchelor (Oxford, Eng.: Lion, 1992), p. 14. (Originally quoted in *New Parish Prayers* by Frank Colquhoun, Hodder & Stoughton Ltd.)

10: Making Sense of Unanswered Prayer

1. Quoted in Roger Steer, *George Müller: Delighted in God* (Wheaton, Ill.: Harold Shaw, 1981), p. 161.

2. C. S. Lewis, *Letters to Malcolm: Chiefly on Prayer* (New York: Harcourt Brace Jovanovich, 1963), p. 59.

3. William Carey, quoted in *The Lord of the Journey*, ed. Roger Pooley and Philip Seddon (London: Collins, 1986), p. 281.

4. Martin Buber, *Dialogue Between Heaven and Earth*, quoted in David Manning White, *Eternal Quest*, vol. 2 (New York: Paragon House, 1992), p. 70.

5. C. S. Lewis, *A Grief Observed* (New York: Bantam Books, 1961), pp. 4–5.

11: Knowing What to Do When Praying Seems Impossible

1. John Donne, *John Donne's Sermons on the Psalms and Gospels*, ed. Evelyn M. Simpson (Berkeley and Los Angeles: University of California Press, 1967), p. 226.

2. Tad Dunne, *We Cannot Find Words* (Denville, N.J.: Dimension Books, 1981), pp. 14–15.

3. Dom John Chapman, quoted in Henri Nouwen, *The Road to Daybreak* (New York: Doubleday, 1988), p. 117.

4. Steve Brown, *Approaching God* (Nashville: Moorings, 1996), p. 46.

5. George Arthur Buttrick, quoted in Richard Foster, *Prayer* (San Francisco: HarperSanFrancisco, 1992), p. 17.

6. Thomas Merton, *Thoughts in Solitude* (Boston: Shambhala, 1956), p. 46.

7. Quoted in George Gallup, Jr., and Timothy Jones, *The Saints Among Us* (Harrisburg, Pa.: Morehouse, 1992), p. 53.

8. David Bolt, quoted in Edythe Draper, *Draper's Book of Quotations for the Christian World* (Wheaton, Ill.: Tyndale, 1992), p. 480.

9. Henri Nouwen, *A Cry for Mercy* (Garden City, N.Y.: Doubleday, 1981), p. 26.

12: Seeking Out Model Prayers

1. Richard Foster, "Growing Edges," *Renovaré Perspective*, October 1996, p. 1.

2. Eugene Peterson, *Answering God* (San Francisco: Harper & Row, 1989), p. 17.

3. Ibid., p. 87.

4. Simon Tugwell, quoted in *The Lord of the Journey*, ed. Roger Pooley and Philip Seddon (London: Collins, 1986), p. 232.

5. Mary Batchelor, ed., *The Lion Prayer Collection* (Oxford, Eng.: Lion, 1992), p. 85.

13: Finding That Two Are Better Than One

1. Eugene H. Peterson, *Answering God* (San Francisco: Harper & Row, 1989), p. 89.

2. Ibid., p. 19.

3. James W. Pennebaker, *Opening Up* (New York: Avon Books, 1990), p. 14.

14: Making Prayer in the Everyday

1. Thomas Kelly, *A Testament of Devotion* (New York: Harper & Row, 1941), p. 39.

2. Martin Marty, quoted in *How I Pray*, ed. Jim Castelli (New York: Ballantine Books, 1994), p. 92.

3. Jean-Pierre de Caussade, *The Sacrament of the Present Moment*, trans. Kitty Muggeridge (San Francisco: Harper & Row, 1981), p. 80.

4. Frederick Buechner, *The Alphabet of Grace* (New York: Walker and Company, 1970), pp. 94–95.

5. Willa Cather, quoted in Dan Wakefield, *Expect a Miracle* (San Francisco: HarperSanFrancisco, 1995), p. 6.

6. Mary Batchelor, ed., *The Lion Prayer Collection* (Oxford, Eng.: Lion, 1992), p. 120.

7. Ibid., p. 118.

15: Letting Go and Being Led

1. Source unknown.

2. Søren Kierkegaard, *The Journals of Søren Kierkegaard*, ed. Alexander Dru (New York: Harper & Brothers, 1959), p. 245, quoted in Richard Foster, *Prayer* (San Francisco: HarperSanFrancisco, 1992), p. 54.

3. Thomas Merton, *Thoughts in Solitude* (Boston: Shambhala, 1993), p. 47.

4. Macrina Wiederkehr, *A Treeful of Angels* (San Francisco: HarperSanFrancisco, 1988), p. 68.

5. Ibid., p. 11.

6. Catherine Marshall, *Adventures in Prayer* (New York: Ballantine Books, 1975), p. 62.

7. Esther de Waal, *Living with Contradiction* (San Francisco: Harper & Row, 1989), p. 93.

8. Quoted in Alan E. Nelson, *Broken in the Right Place* (Nashville: Thomas Nelson Publishers, 1993), pp. 88–89.

9. Catherine Marshall, *Adventures in Prayer*, pp. 70–71.

16: Moving Forward

1. V. Donovan, quoted in *The Lord of the Journey*, ed. Roger Pooley and Philip Seddon (London: Collins, 1986), pp. 118–19.

2. Thomas Kelly, *A Testament of Devotion* (New York: Harper & Row, 1941), p. 281.

3. Ibid., p. 45.

4. John Cassian, *Conferences* (The Classics of Western Spirituality) (New York: Paulist Press, 1985), p. 116.

5. Saint Augustine, *Confessions* (Oxford, Eng.: Oxford University Press, 1991), p. 201.

6. Harold Myra, *Living by God's Surprises* (Waco, Tex.: Word, 1988).

7. C. S. Lewis, *The Lion, the Witch and the Wardrobe* (New York: Collier/Macmillan, 1950), pp. 75–76.

Index

Dossey, Larry, 8
Dryness, in prayer,
171–173
Dunne, Tad, 164

Ecclesiastes 3:1,7, 48
Ecclesiastes 4:9–10, 197
Ecclesiastes 4:9–11, 188
Eli, 138
Emotions, in prayer,
121–132
Ephesians 3:12, 85
Ephesians 6:11, 175
Everyday life, prayer in,
166, 199–209
Evil, 79–82, 84, 157–158,
160, 174–177,
193
Exodus 4:10, 34
Exodus 32:9–14, 107
Exodus 33:11, 34

Fafinski, John, 53
Failings, facing, 71–86
Fasting, 168
Faulkner, William, 42
Fénelon, François, 39
Forgiveness, 73, 85–86
Foster, Richard, 41–42,
122, 127, 179–180
Frankfurt Prayer, 55
Franny and Zooey
(Salinger), 53

Galli, Mark, 43–44
Galloway, Dale, 218–219
Gift, prayer as, 225–230
Giles, Brother, 18–19
Graham, Billy, 134
Grief Observed, A (Lewis),
158
Guilt, 72, 73, 79, 80,
83–85

Habakkuk 2:20, 51
*Healing Words: The Power
of Prayer and the
Practice of Medicine*
(Dossey), 8
Hebrews 4:12, 176
Herbert, George, 61, 209
Holmes, Oliver Wendell,
40
Holocaust, 157
Hope, 85, 93, 116
Humility, 75, 213
Hunger, 9
Hunter, Jeanie, 154–156

Images of God, 62–67
Incompleteness, 75–78
Ingelow, Jean, 146
Intercession, 112–115,
186
Isaac the Syrian, 82
Isaiah 6:1, 5, 82
Isaiah 30:15, 40

About the Author

TIMOTHY JONES is a freelance writer and editor. Until recently he was managing editor for Moorings, a Nashville-based division of the Ballantine Publishing Group that specializes in publishing Christian books. For almost six years before joining Moorings, Timothy was an editor at *Christianity Today* magazine. Before that he was a pastor for almost eight years. He graduated with a master's degree from Princeton Theological Seminary in 1979. He has written other books, including *Celebration of Angels*, *The Friendship Connection: How Mentors and Friends Can Make Your Faith Strong*, and *The Saints Among Us*, coauthored with pollster George Gallup, Jr. He lives in the Nashville, Tennessee, area with his wife, Jill, and their three children.